For Engineers & Designers

ANSYS 3D Exercises

200 3D PRACTICE DRAWINGS

SACHIDANAND JHA

Dear Reader,

Thank you for choosing **ANSYS 3D Exercises** book. This book is part of a family of premium-quality CADIN360 books, all of which are written by Outstanding author who combine practical experience with a gift for teaching.

CADIN360 was founded in 2016. More than 3 years later, we're still committed to producing consistently exceptional books. With each of our titles, we're working hard to set a new standard for the industry. From the paper we print on, to the authors we work with, our goal is to bring you the best books available.

I hope you see all that reflected in these pages. I'd be very interested to hear your comments and get your feedback on how we're doing. Feel free to let me know what you think about this or any other CADIN360 book by sending me an email at contactus@cadin360.com.

If you think you've found a technical error in this book, please visit https://cadin360.com/contact-us/.
Customer feedback is critical to our efforts at CADIN360.

Best regards,

Sachidanand Jha
Founder & CEO, CADIN360

ANSYS 3D Exercises

Published by
CADIN360
cadin360.com

Limit of Liability/Disclaimer of Warranty:

Examination Copies

Electronic Files

Disclaimer:

Preface

ANSYS 3D Exercises

❖ This book contain 200 CAD practice exercises and drawings.

❖ This book does not provide step by step tutorial to design 3D models.

❖ S.I Unit is used.

❖ Predominantly used Third Angle Projection.

❖ This book is for **ANSYS** and Other Feature-Based Modeling Software such as Inventor, SolidWorks, NX, Solid Edge, AutoCAD, PTC Creo etc.

❖ It is intended to provide Drafters, Designers and Engineers with enough 3D CAD exercises for practice on **ANSYS.**

❖ It includes almost all types of exercises that are necessary to provide, clear, concise and systematic information required on industrial machine part drawings.

❖ Third Angle Projection is intentionally used to familiarize Drafters, Designers and Engineers in Third Angle Projection to meet the expectation of world wide Engineering drawing print.

❖ Clear and well drafted drawing help easy understanding of the design.

❖ This book is for Beginner, Intermediate and Advance CAD users.

❖ These exercises are from Basics to Advance level.

❖ Each exercises can be assigned and designed separately.

❖ No Exercise is a prerequisite for another. All dimensions are in mm.

❖ Note: Assume any missing dimensions.

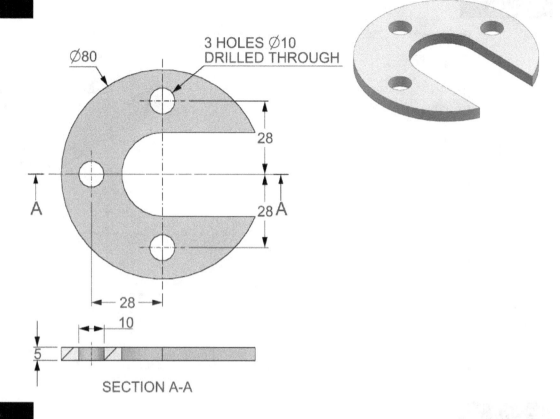

Ø80
3 HOLES Ø10
DRILLED THROUGH

28
28 A
A
28
10
5
SECTION A-A

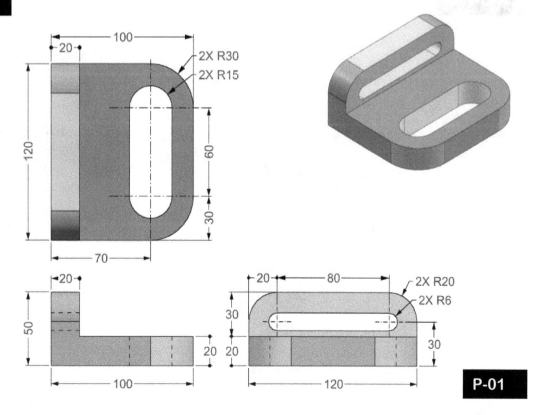

100
20
2X R30
2X R15
120
60
30
70
20
50
20 20
100
20 80
2X R20
2X R6
30
30
120

EX-03

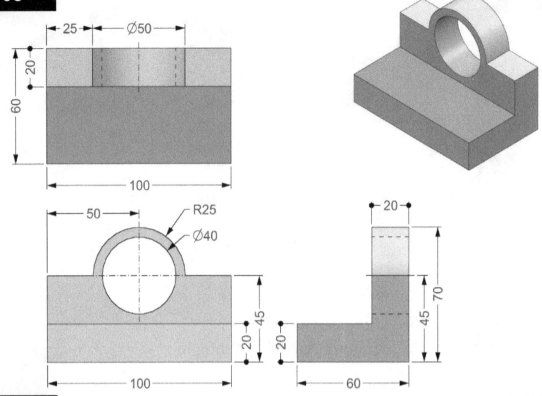

25 | Ø50 | 20 | 60 | 100

50 | R25 | Ø40 | 45 | 20 | 20 | 100 | 20 | 70 | 45 | 60

EX-04

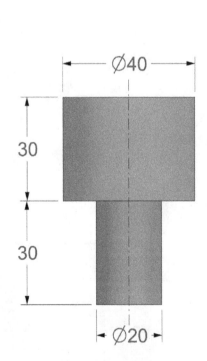

Ø40 | 30 | 30 | Ø20

P-02

EX-05

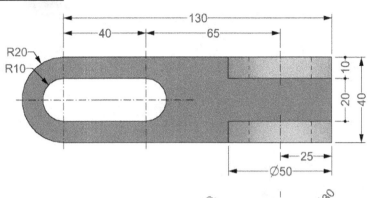

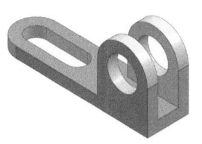

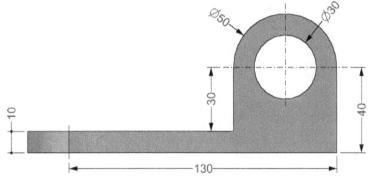

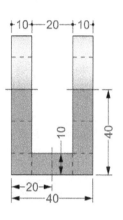

EX-06

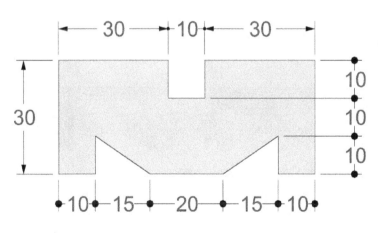

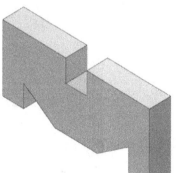

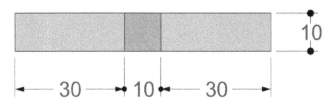

P-03

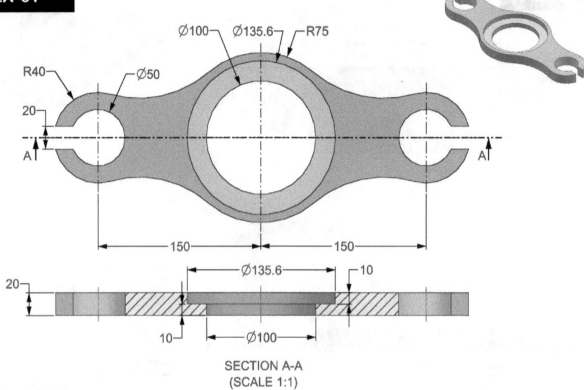

Ø100 — Ø135.6 — R75

R40 —
Ø50

20 —
A

A

150 — 150

Ø135.6 — 10

20 —

10 — Ø100

SECTION A-A
(SCALE 1:1)

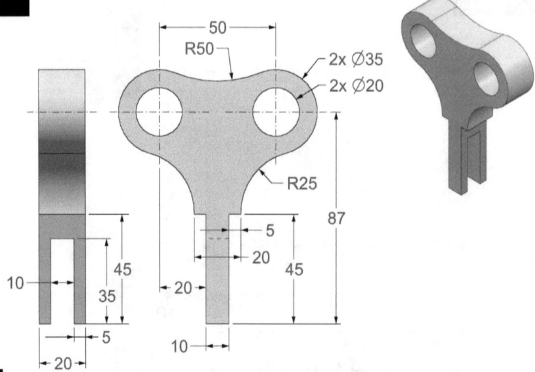

50
R50 —
2x Ø35
2x Ø20

R25

87

5
20
45

45

10 —

20 —
20 —

10 —

10
35
5
20

EX-09

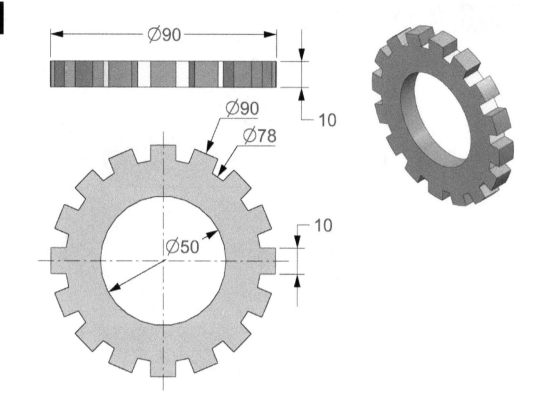

Ø90

10

Ø90
Ø78
Ø50
10

EX-10

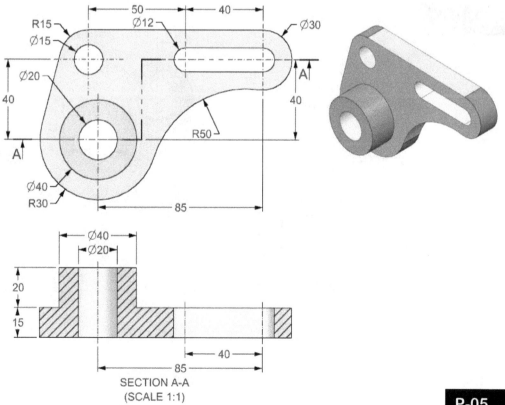

R15
Ø15
Ø20
Ø12
Ø30
40
A
40
R50
85
A
Ø40
R30
50   40

Ø40
Ø20
20
15
40
85

SECTION A-A
(SCALE 1:1)

P-05

EX-11

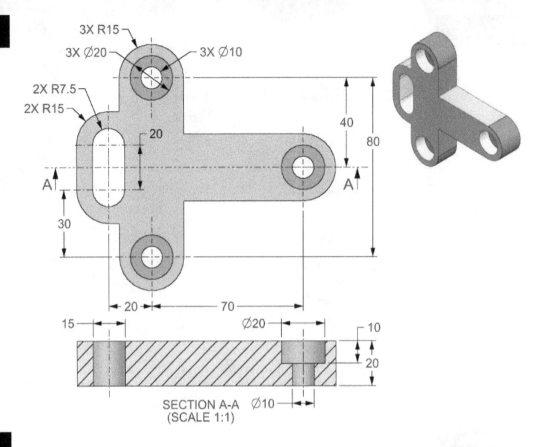

3X R15
3X Ø20
3X Ø10
2X R7.5
2X R15
20
40
80
30
20
70

15
Ø20
10
20
SECTION A-A
(SCALE 1:1)
Ø10

EX-12

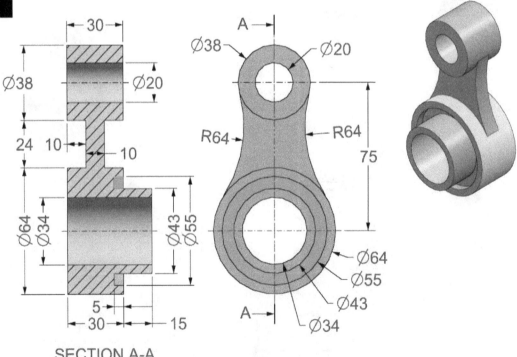

30
Ø38
Ø20
24 10
10
Ø64
Ø34
Ø43
Ø55
5
30
15

A
Ø38
Ø20
R64
R64
75
Ø64
Ø55
Ø43
Ø34
A

SECTION A-A
(SCALE 1:1)

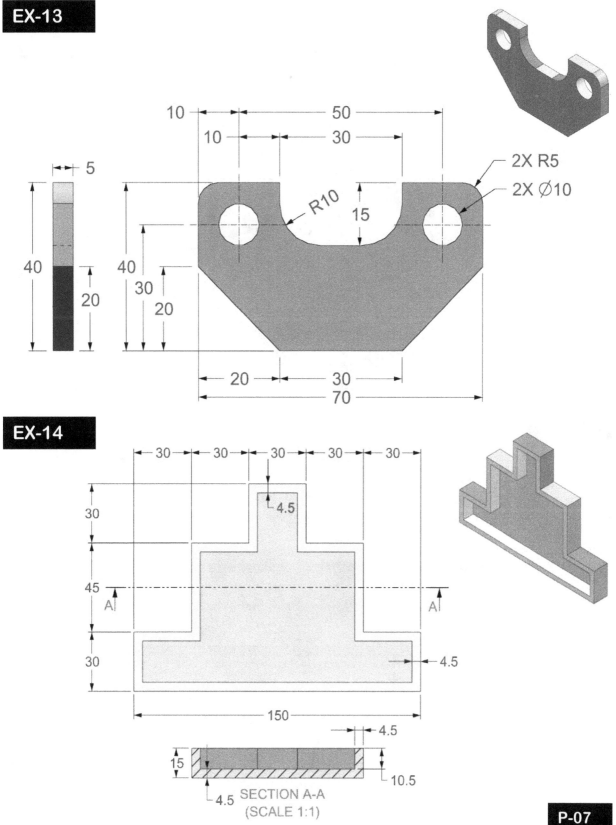

2X R5
2X Ø10
R10

SECTION A-A
(SCALE 1:1)

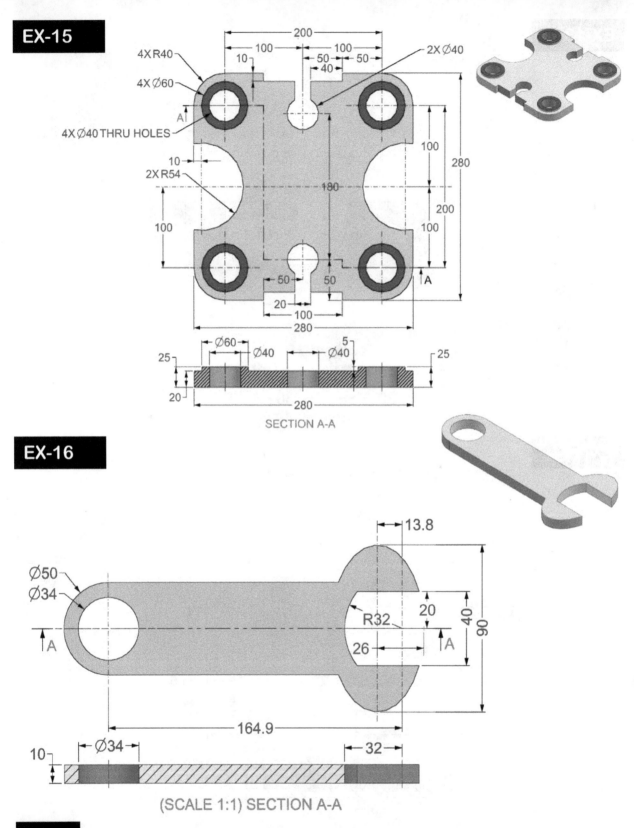

EX-15

4X R40
4X Ø60
4X Ø40 THRU HOLES
2X R54

200
100 100
10
50 50
40
2X Ø40

A

10
100
280
180
200
100
100

50 50
20
100
280

SECTION A-A

Ø60
Ø40
Ø40
5
25
20
280
25

EX-16

Ø50
Ø34

13.8
R32
20
40
90
26
A

164.9

10
Ø34
32

(SCALE 1:1) SECTION A-A

P-08

EX-17

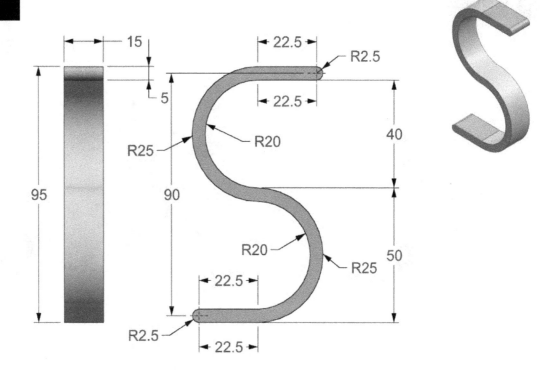

15
22.5
R2.5
22.5
5
R25
R20
40
95
90
R20
50
R25
22.5
R2.5
22.5
22.5

EX-18

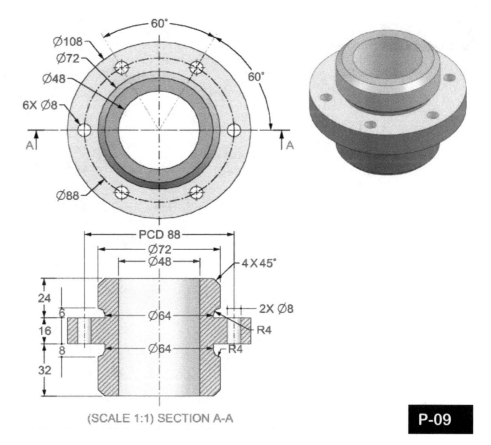

60°
Ø108
Ø72
60°
Ø48
6X Ø8
Ø88

PCD 88
Ø72
Ø48
4 X 45°
24
6
Ø64
2X Ø8
16
R4
8
Ø64
R4
32

(SCALE 1:1) SECTION A-A

P-09

EX-19

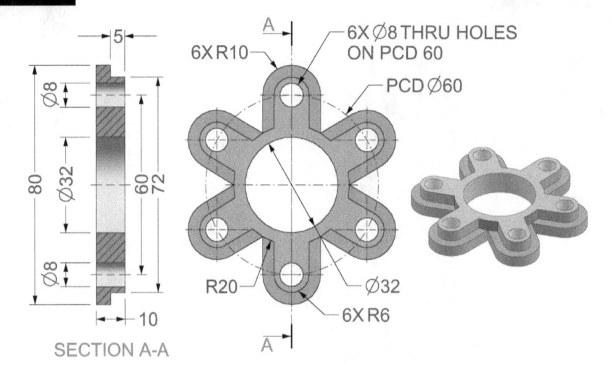

5

Ø8

Ø32

80

60

72

Ø8

10

SECTION A-A

A

6X R10

6X Ø8 THRU HOLES ON PCD 60

PCD Ø60

R20

Ø32

6X R6

A

EX-20

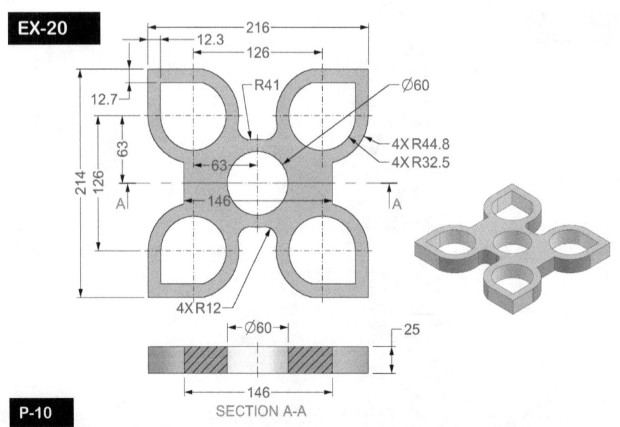

216

12.3

126

R41

Ø60

12.7

63

214

126

63

4X R44.8

4X R32.5

A

146

A

4X R12

Ø60

25

146

SECTION A-A

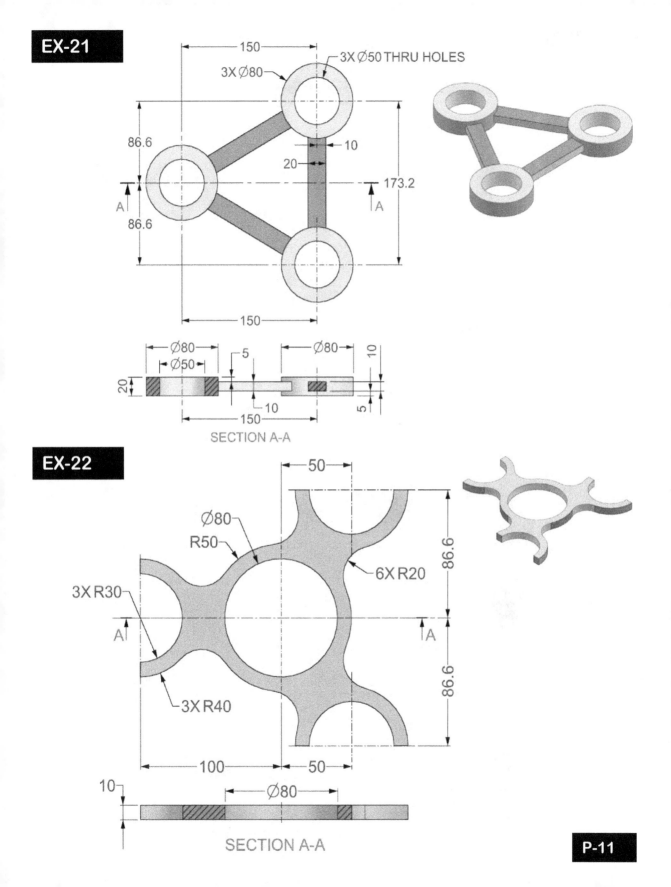

EX-21

150
3X Ø50 THRU HOLES
3X Ø80
86.6
10
20
173.2
A
A
86.6
150

Ø80
Ø50
5
Ø80
10
20
10
5
150
SECTION A-A

EX-22

50
Ø80
R50
86.6
6X R20
3X R30
A
A
86.6
3X R40
100
50

10
Ø80
SECTION A-A

P-11

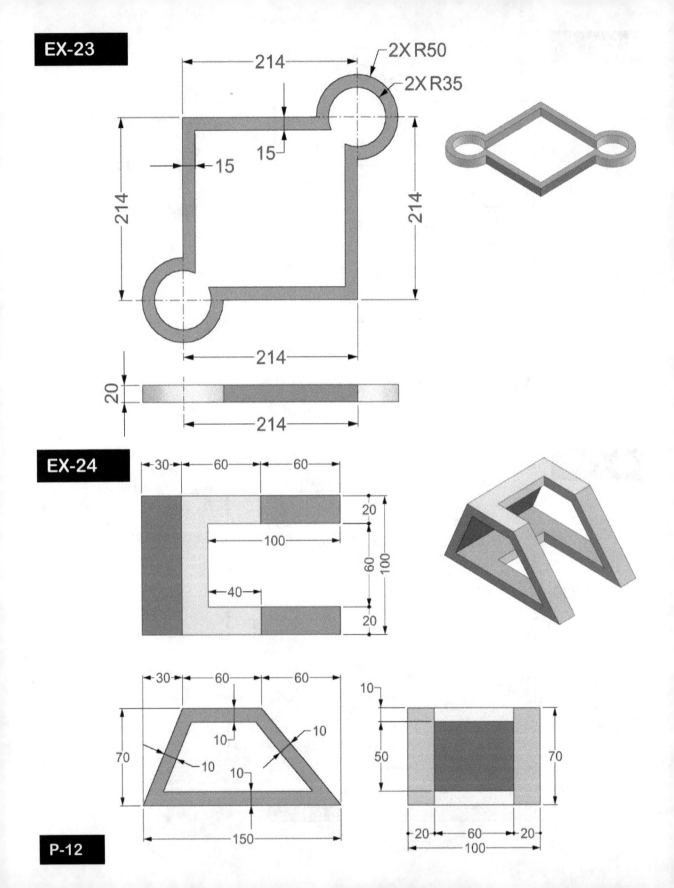

EX-23

2X R50
2X R35
214
15
15
214
214
214
214
20
214

EX-24

30 · 60 · 60
20
100
60 · 100
40
20

30 · 60 · 60
70
10
10
10
10
150

10
50
70
20 · 60 · 20
100

P-12

EX-25

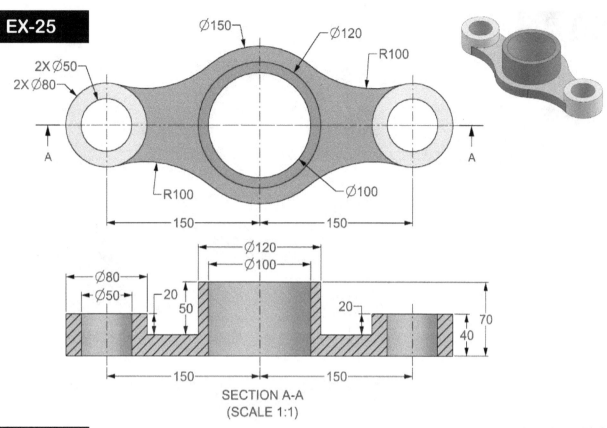

Ø150
Ø120
R100
2X Ø50
2X Ø80
R100
Ø100
150 150

Ø120
Ø100
Ø80
Ø50
20
50
20
70
40
150 150

SECTION A-A
(SCALE 1:1)

EX-26

Ø24
Ø44
Ø36

A A

Ø44
Ø36
Ø32
Ø24
2X45°
12
8
36
12
4
3

SECTION A-A
(SCALE 1:1)

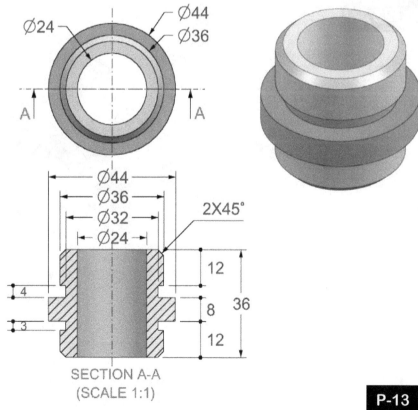

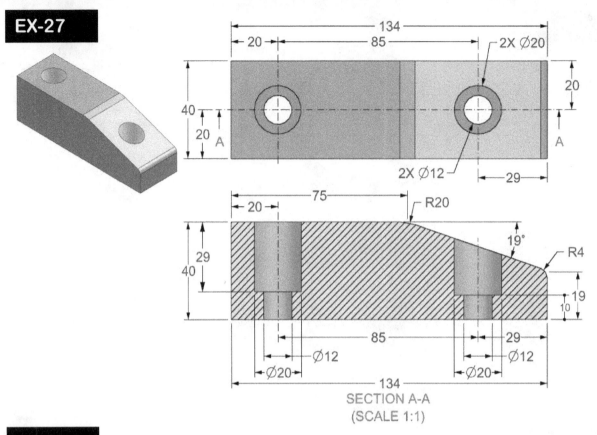

134
20
85
2X ∅20
40
20
20
A
A
2X ∅12
29

75
R20
20
19°
29
R4
40
19
10
∅12
∅20
85
29
∅12
∅20
134
SECTION A-A
(SCALE 1:1)

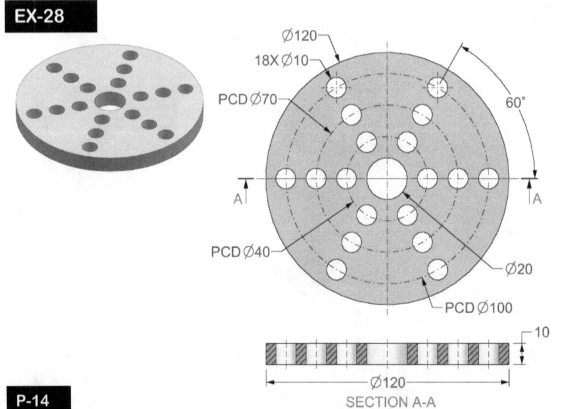

∅120
18X ∅10
PCD ∅70
60°
PCD ∅40
∅20
PCD ∅100
A
A
10
∅120
SECTION A-A

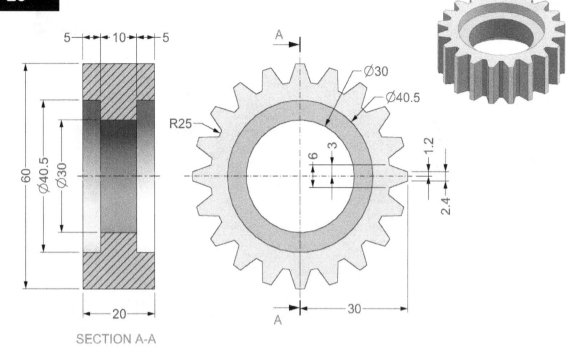

SECTION A-A

Ø30
Ø40.5
R25
6
3
1.2
2.4
30
60
Ø40.5
Ø30
5
10
5
20

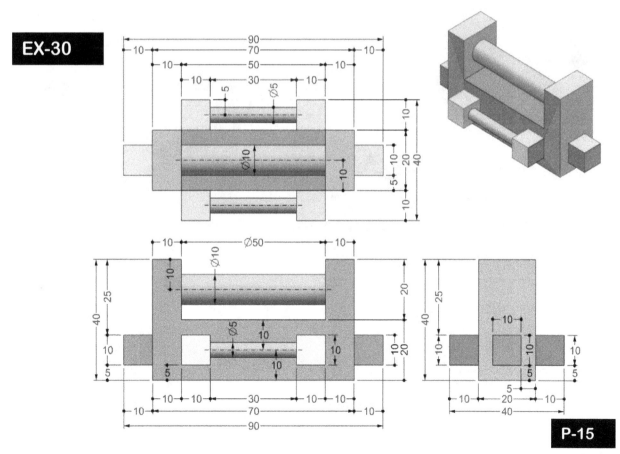

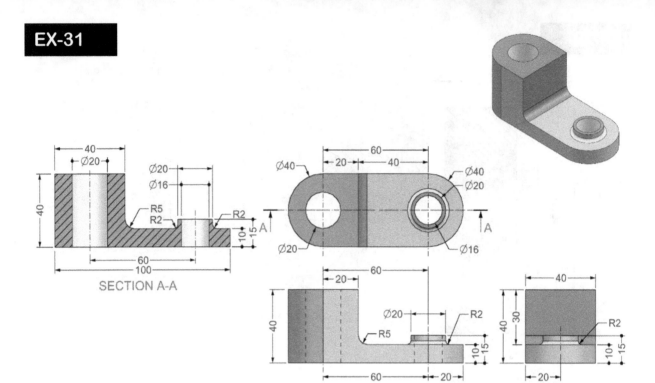

SECTION A-A

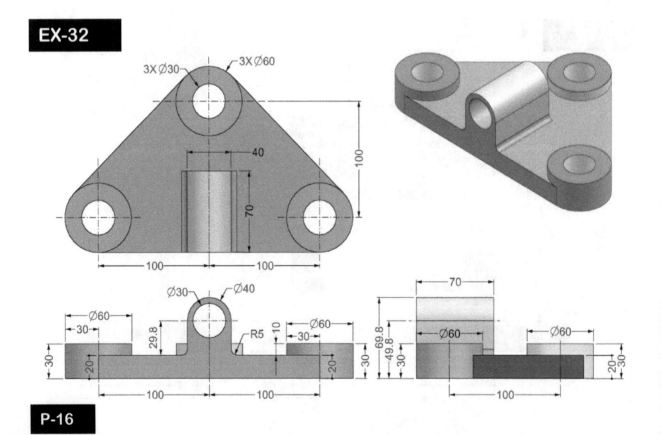

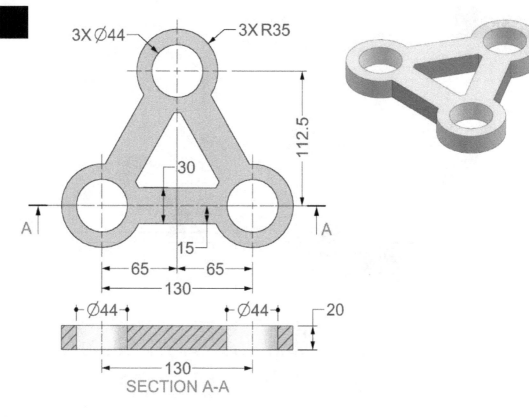

3X ⌀44 — 3X R35

112.5

30

A | A

15

65 — 65

130

⌀44 — ⌀44 — 20

130

SECTION A-A

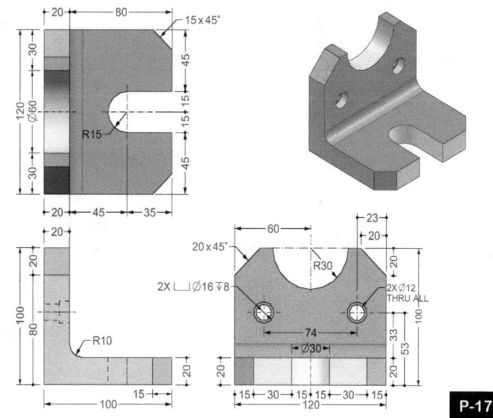

20 — 80 — 15 x 45°

30

45

120 ⌀60 15

15

30 45

20 — 45 — 35

20

20

100 80

R10

15

100

60 — 23

20 x 45° — 20

R30

20

2X ⌣ ⌀16 ▽8 — 2X ⌀12 THRU ALL

74 — 100

33

⌀30 — 53

20

15 — 30 — 15 15 — 30 — 15

120

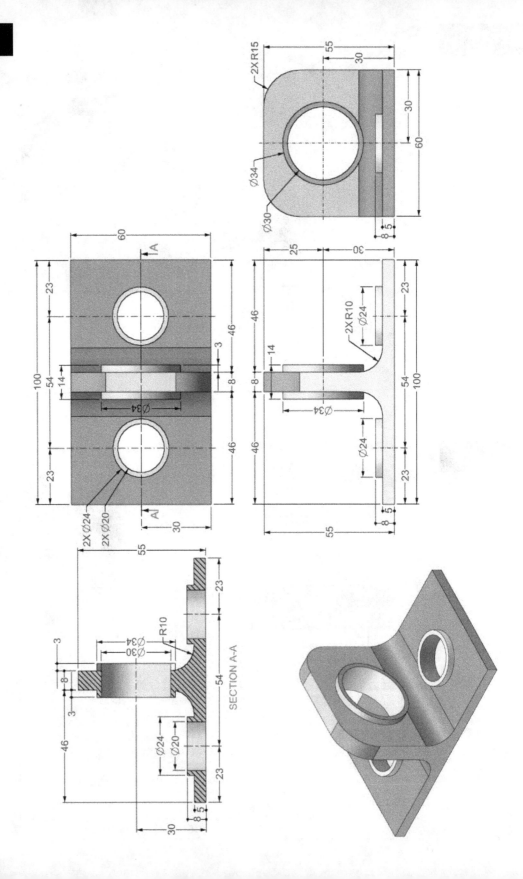

SECTION A-A

2X R15

55
30
30
60

Ø34
Ø30

8
5

25
30

2X R10
Ø24
46
14
8
54
100
46
23
Ø34
Ø24
23

8
5
55

60

A

23
100
54
14
3
8
Ø34
46
46
23

2X Ø24
2X Ø20

A
30

55
23
3
Ø34
Ø30
R10
54
8
3
46
Ø24
Ø20
23
8
5
30

EX-36

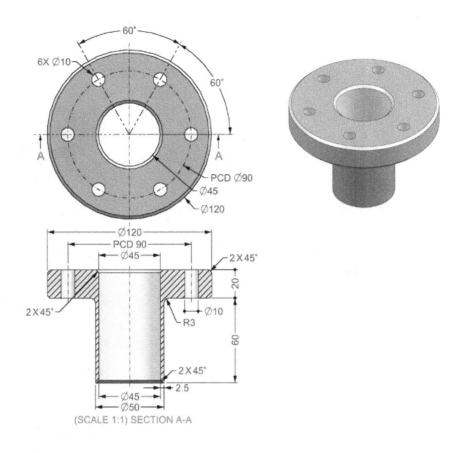

6X Ø10

60°

60°

PCD Ø90
Ø45
Ø120

Ø120
PCD 90
Ø45
2 X 45°
20
2 X 45°
Ø10
R3
60
2 X 45°
2.5
Ø45
Ø50

(SCALE 1:1) SECTION A-A

EX-37

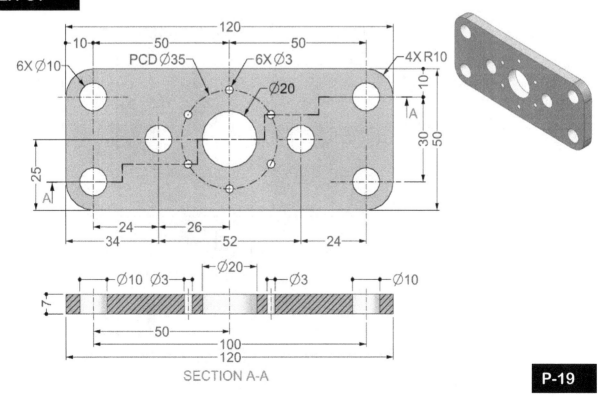

120
10
50
50
6X Ø10
PCD Ø35
6X Ø3
4X R10
Ø20
10
A
30
50
25
A
24
26
34
52
24

Ø20
Ø10 Ø3
Ø3
Ø10
7
50
100
120

SECTION A-A

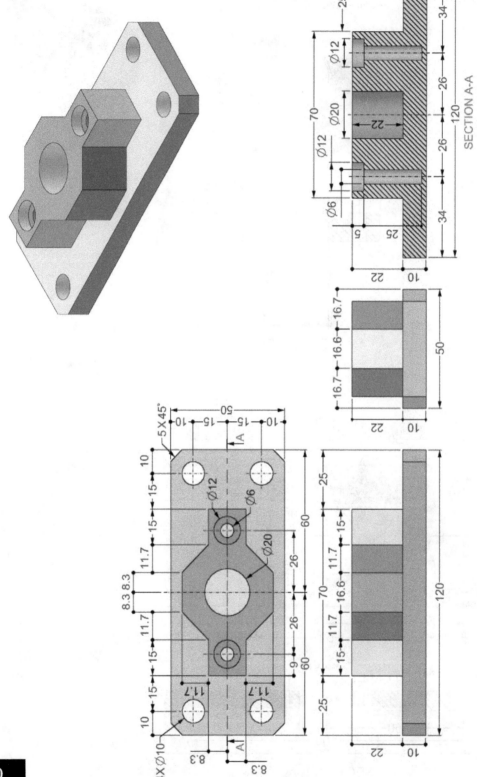

SECTION A-A

EX-39

70

R20

Ø20

40

45

45

R25

Ø20

20

30

10

10

A

A

45

65

20

2X R10

Ø40

Ø20

25

45

SECTION A-A

EX-40

Ø60

20

10

5

Ø50

Ø60

Ø50

5 10 5

30

Ø60

20

P-21

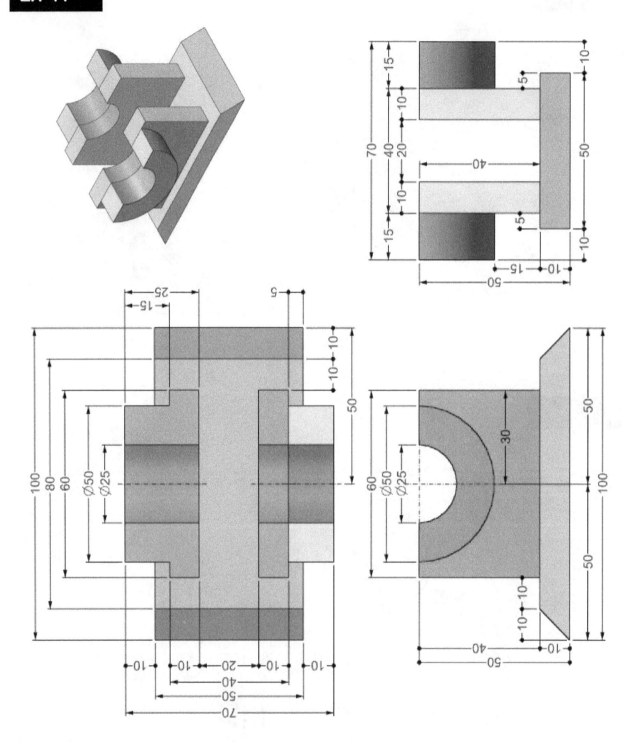

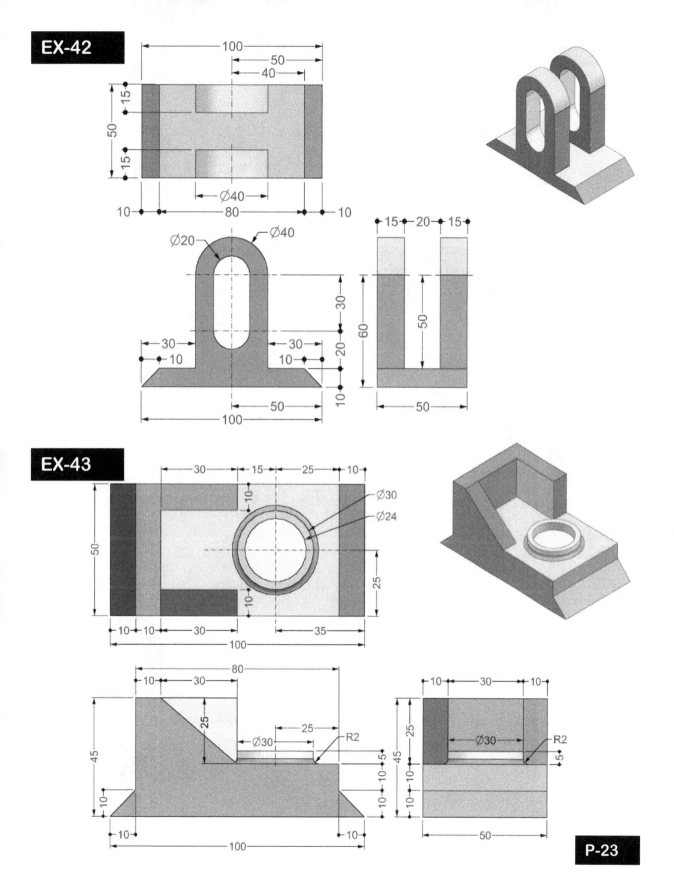

EX-42

EX-43

P-23

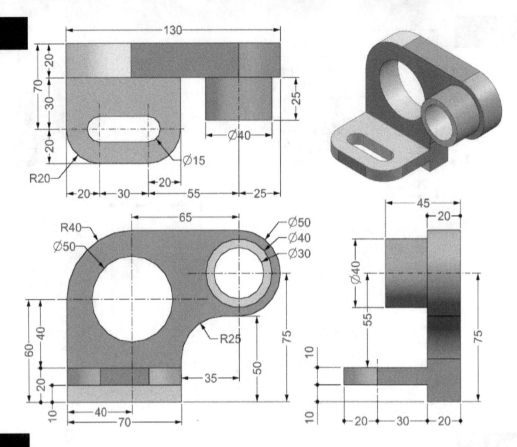

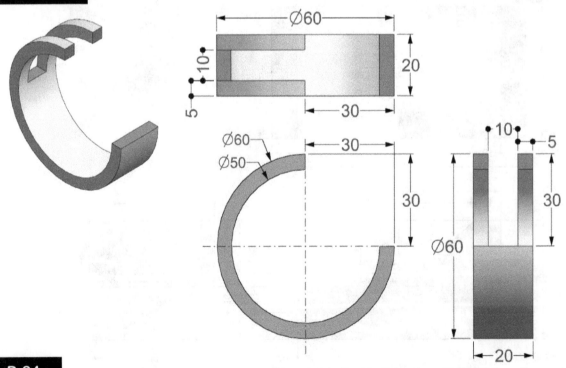

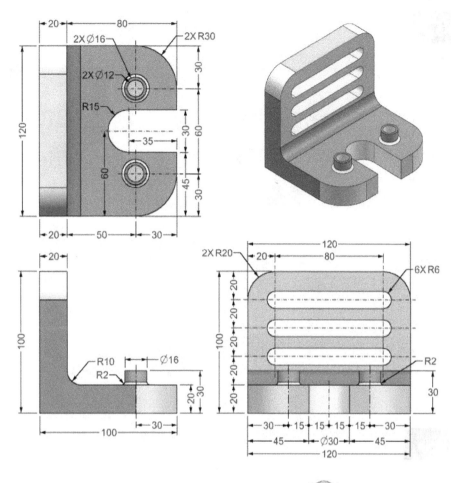

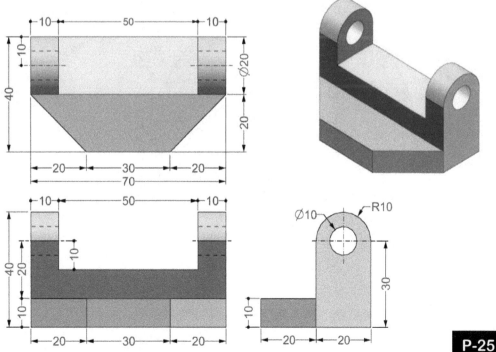

EX-48

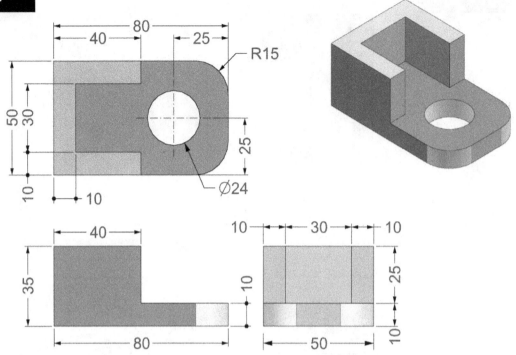

EX-49

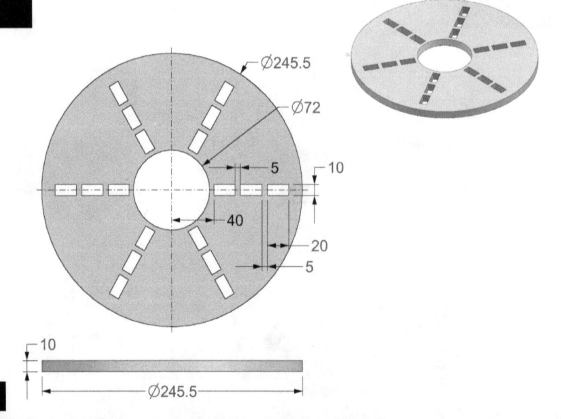

P-26

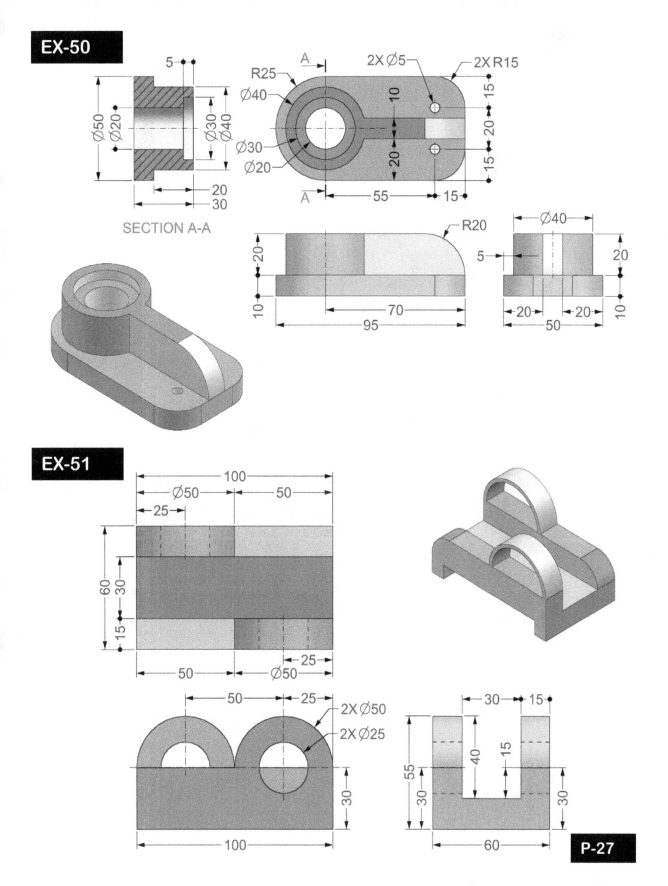

EX-50

5
Ø50
Ø20
Ø30
Ø40
20
30

SECTION A-A

A
R25
Ø40
Ø30
Ø20
2X Ø5
2X R15
10
15
20
15
20
55
15

R20
20
10
70
95

Ø40
5
20
20
50
20
10

EX-51

100
Ø50
50
25
60
30
15
50
25
Ø50

50
25
2X Ø50
2X Ø25
30
100

30
15
55
40
15
30
30
60

P-27

EX-52

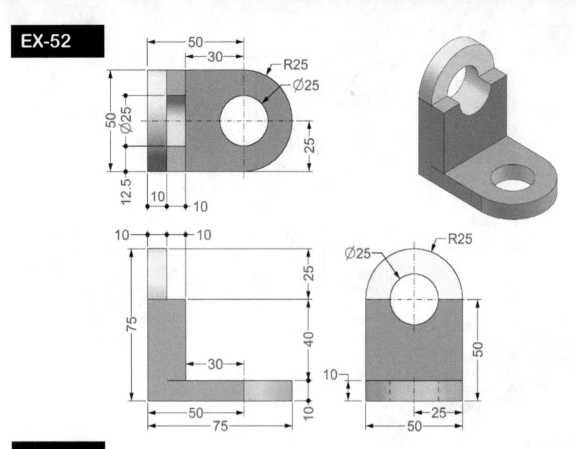

EX-53

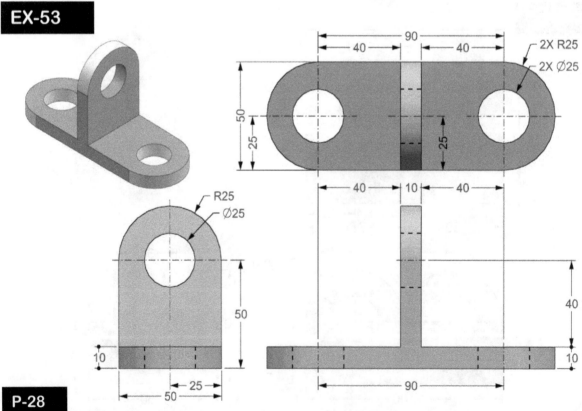

P-28

EX-54

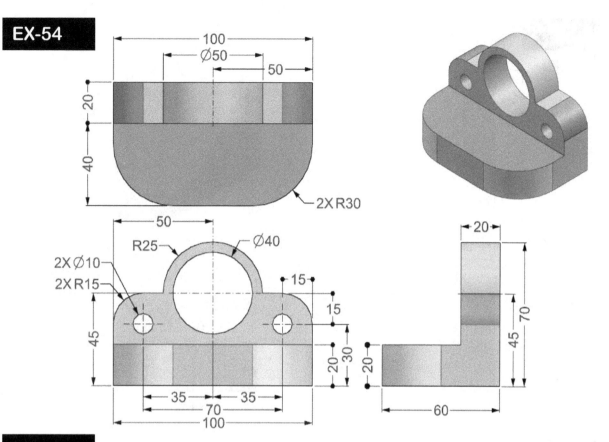

EX-55

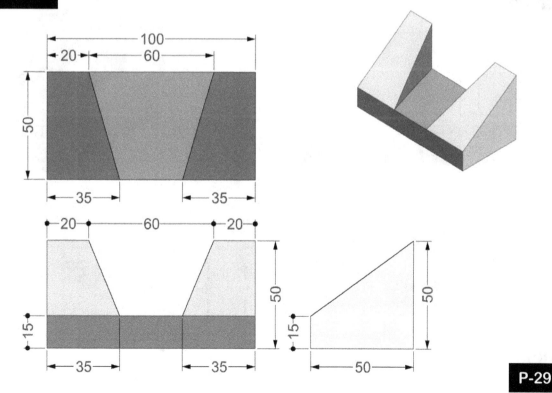

P-29

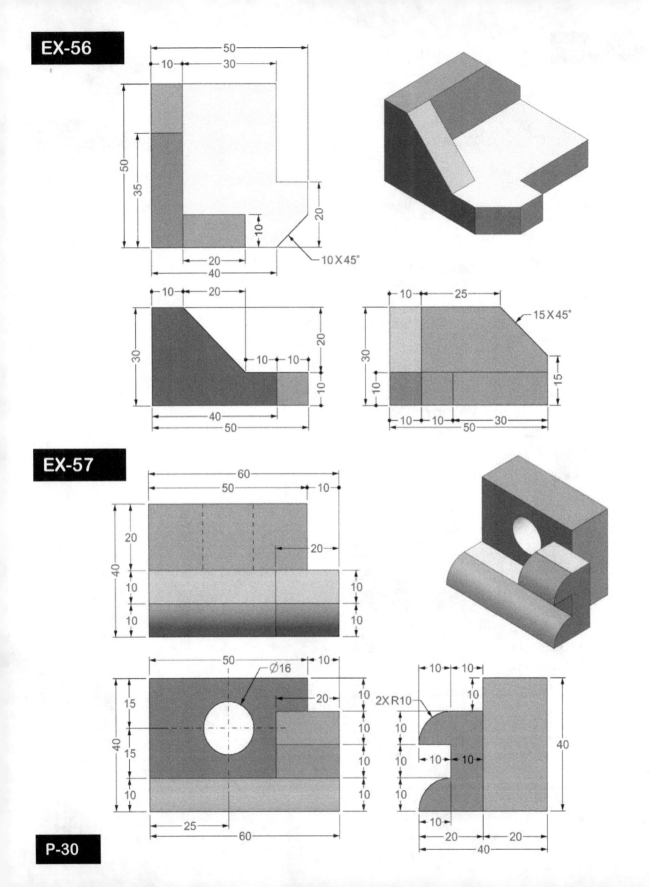

EX-56

EX-57

P-30

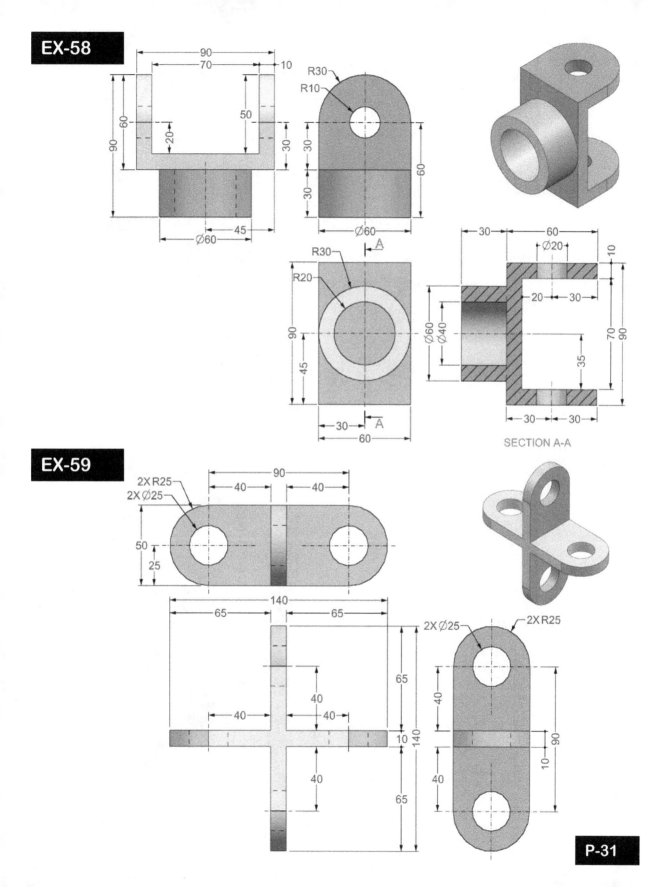

EX-58

R30
R10
Ø60
90
70
10
60
50
20
30
30
45
Ø60

R30
R20
90
45
30
60
A

30
60
Ø20
10
20
30
Ø60
Ø40
70
90
35
30
30

SECTION A-A

EX-59

2X R25
2X Ø25
90
40
40
50
25

140
65
65
65
40
40
10
140
40
65

2X Ø25
2X R25
40
90
10
40

P-31

EX-60

Ø50
22.5
2X Ø10
15
25
43.9
10
60
10
15
25
50
45
95

Ø50
Ø40
R4
R10
R10
10
40
R10
R10
10
45
45
155
130
80
140
R10
R10
30
55
40
10
10
22.5
22.5
100

60
85.4
100
155
34.6
10
25
40
60

EX-61

Ø120
20
R3
50
Ø50
R2
10 10 10
Ø50
Ø70

14 14
PCD Ø90
R60
Ø70
Ø30
Ø50
6X Ø10
66
132
14 14
14 14
A
A
66
66 66
132

132
Ø70
Ø50
Ø30
Ø10
10 10 10
R2
Ø50
Ø30
50
100
R3
Ø10
45 90 45
90
Ø120
20

SECTION A-A

Ø120
PCD Ø90
6X Ø10
ON PCD 90
Ø30
66
132
14 14
66
14 14
66 66
132

P-32

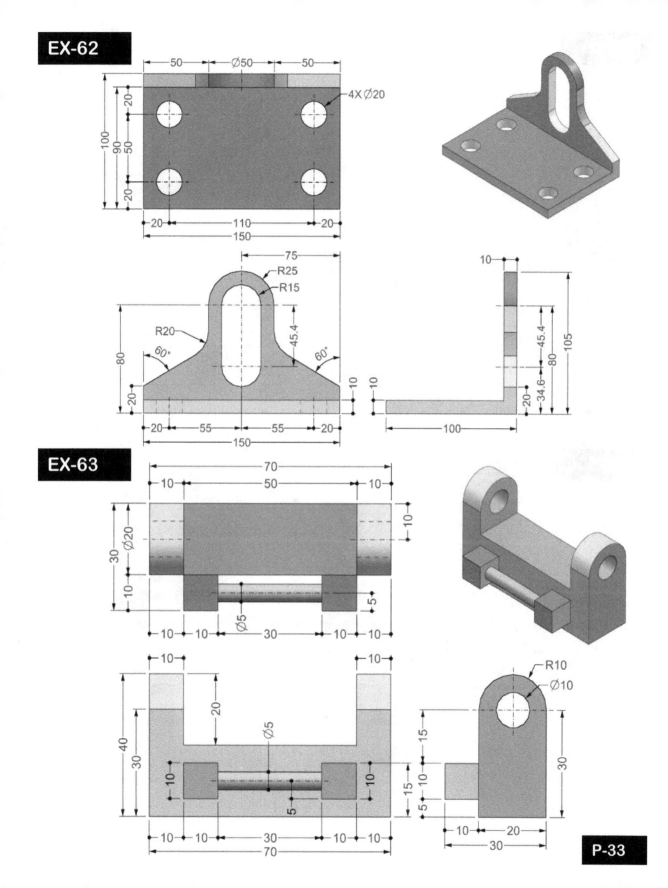

EX-62

EX-63

P-33

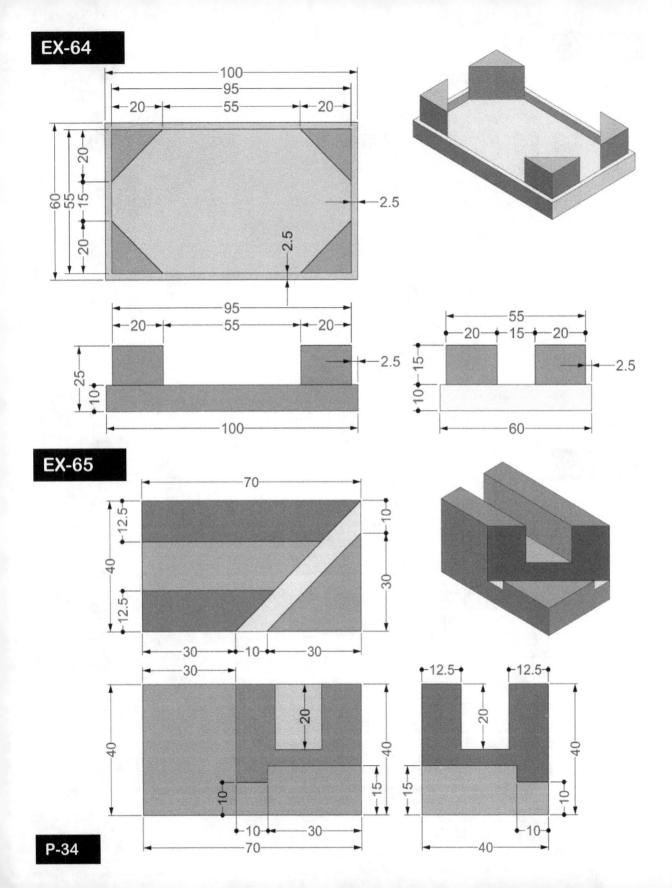

EX-64

EX-65

P-34

EX-66

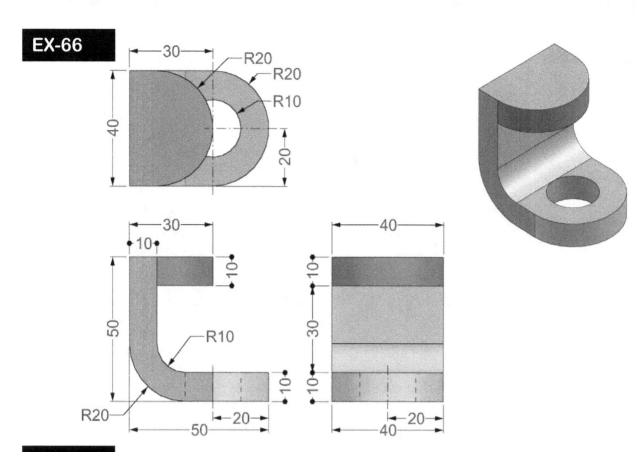

30
R20
R20
R10
40
20

30
10
10
50
R10
R20
50
20
10

40
10
30
10
20
40

EX-67

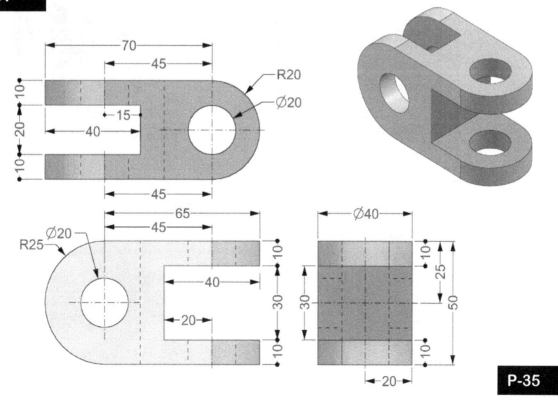

70
45
R20
Ø20
10
20
15
40
10
45

65
45
Ø20
R25
40
20
10
30
10

Ø40
10
25
50
30
10
20

P-35

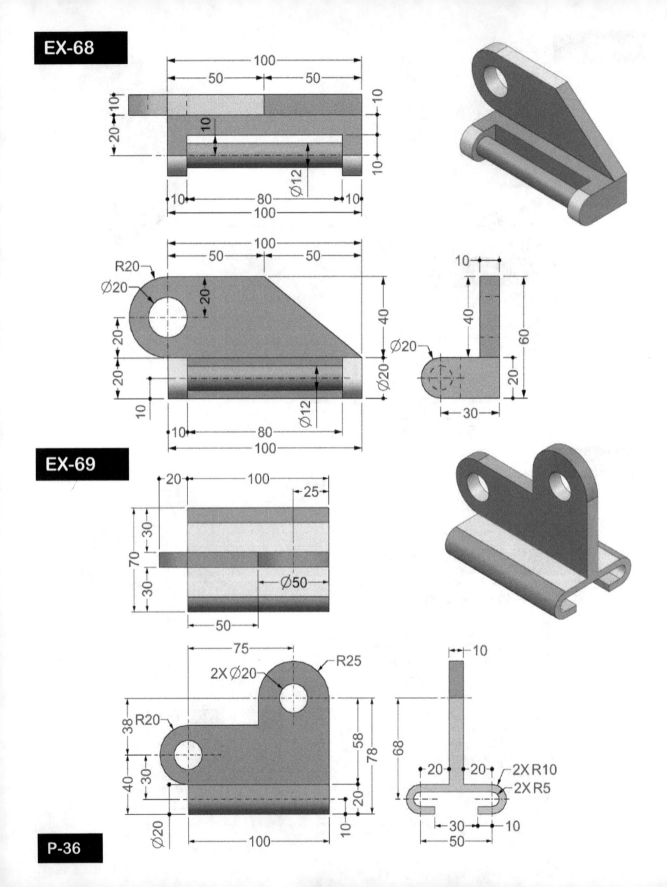

EX-68

EX-69

P-36

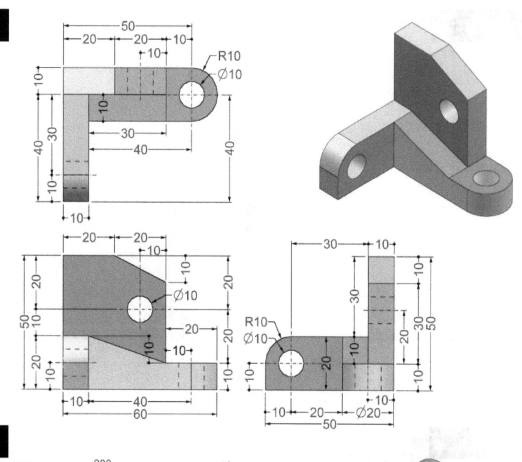

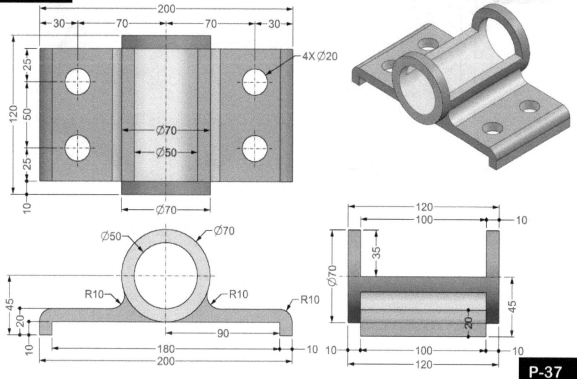

EX-72

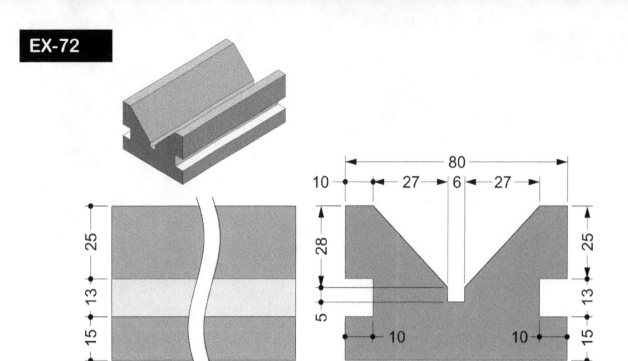

EX-73

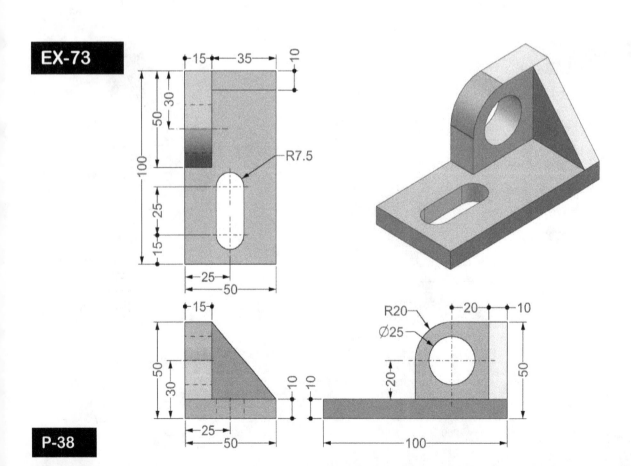

EX-74

4X R10

75 75
10
20
50 110
20
110
10
20 55 55 20
150
Ø50

2X R15 R25
50 50
R20
45.4
34.6
120°
20
75 75
150

10 90 10
60
10
20
45.4
34.6
20
110

EX-75

40
Ø60
120
90
20
60

40
Ø60
50
20 7.5
15
15 30
60

90
Ø60
Ø40
65
15
120

120
70
R20
Ø28
10
40
20
40
10
50

70
R25
10
Ø30
15
15
10
50
70

25
20
Ø40

R15
R25
50
R10
A
A
R5

Ø30
50
R1
30
30
20
30
R4
R2
Ø10
5

SECTION A-A

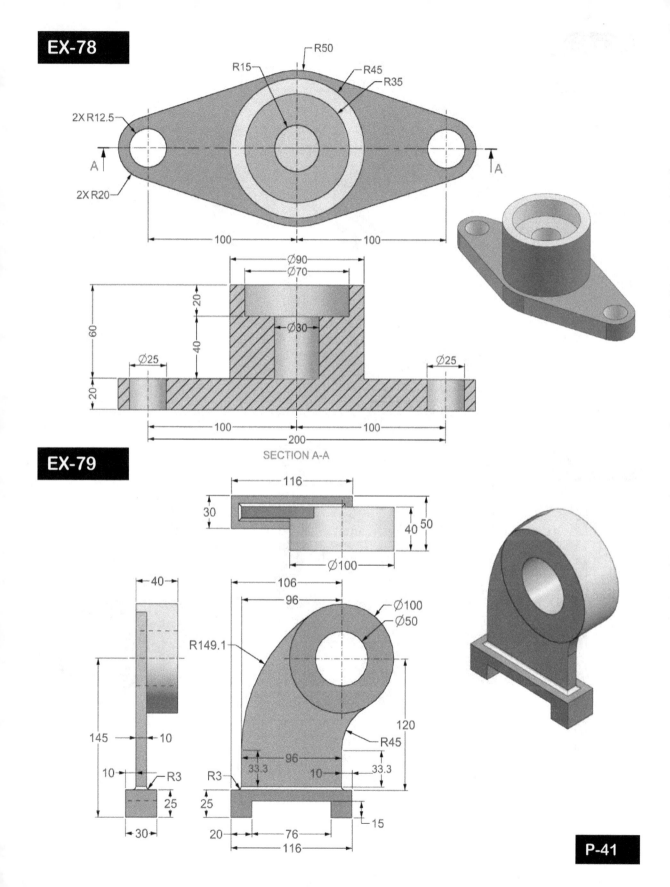

EX-78

2X R12.5

2X R20

R15
R50
R45
R35

A
A

100
100

∅90
∅70
20
40
∅30
60

∅25
∅25
20

100
100
200

SECTION A-A

EX-79

116
30
40 50
∅100

40
106
96
∅100
∅50
R149.1

145 — 10
10 — R3
25
30

R3
33.3
96
10
33.3

R45
120

25
20
76
116
15

P-41

EX-80

6 HOLES, Ø10
ON DIA 32 PCD

4 HOLES, Ø8.6
ON DIA 54 PCD

Ø70

Ø16

A

A

Ø54

Ø32

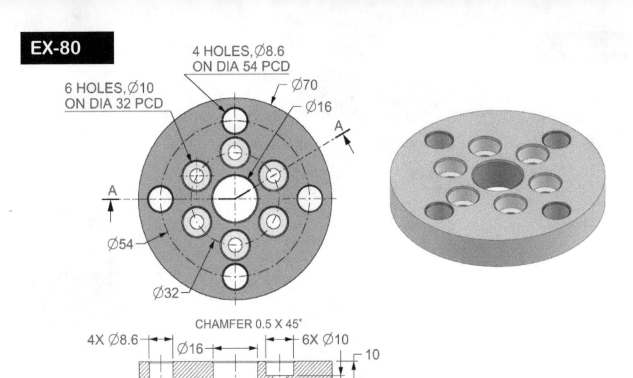

CHAMFER 0.5 X 45°

4X Ø8.6

Ø16

6X Ø10

10

5

5

SECTION A-A
(SCALE 1:1)

EX-81

207.2

171.6

17.8

10

6X Ø8.4

87.2

4X R19.4

19.2

9.6

106

254

233.6

190.4

254

109.8

36.6

56.4

38 28

2X R11.6

10

60

10

103.6

147.2

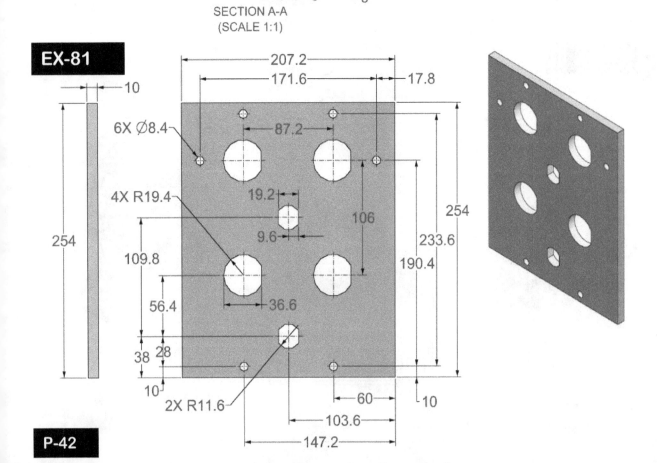

P-42

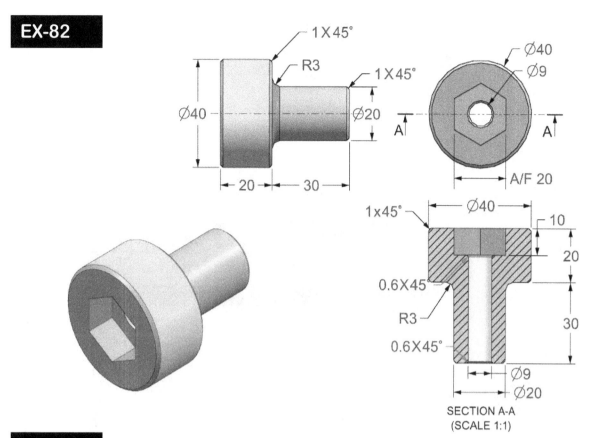

1X45°
R3
1X45°
Ø40
Ø9
Ø40
Ø20
A
A
A/F 20
20
30

Ø40
1x45°
10
20
0.6X45°
R3
30
0.6X45°
Ø9
Ø20

SECTION A-A
(SCALE 1:1)

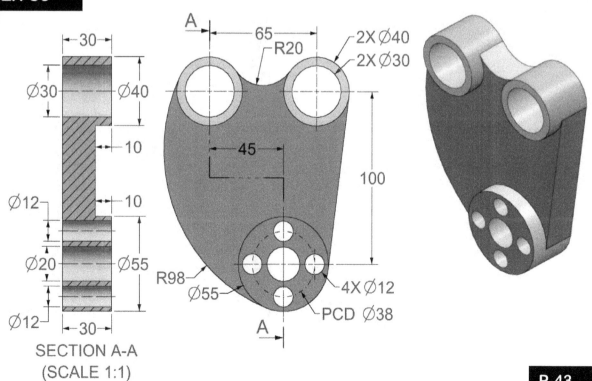

30
Ø30
Ø40
10
10
Ø12
Ø20
Ø55
Ø12
30

SECTION A-A
(SCALE 1:1)

A
65
R20
2X Ø40
2X Ø30
45
100
R98
Ø55
4X Ø12
PCD Ø38
A

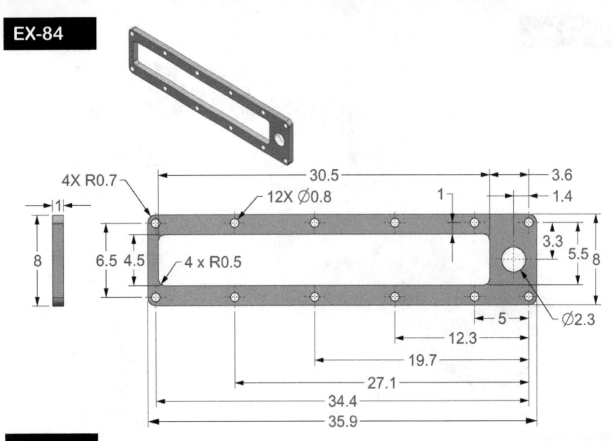

4X R0.7
12X Ø0.8
30.5
3.6
1.4
1
1
8
4X R0.5
6.5 4.5
3.3
5.5 8
Ø2.3
5
12.3
19.7
27.1
34.4
35.9

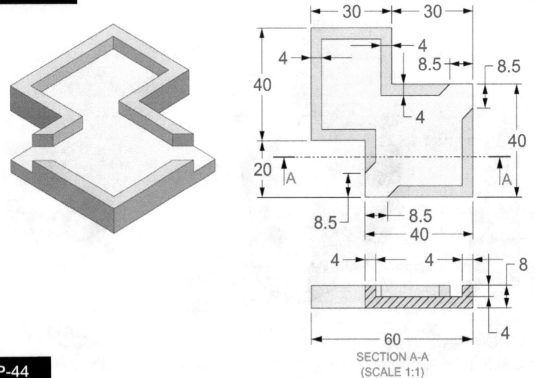

30
30
4
4
8.5
8.5
4
40
4
40
20
A
A
8.5
8.5
40
4
4
8
60
4
SECTION A-A
(SCALE 1:1)

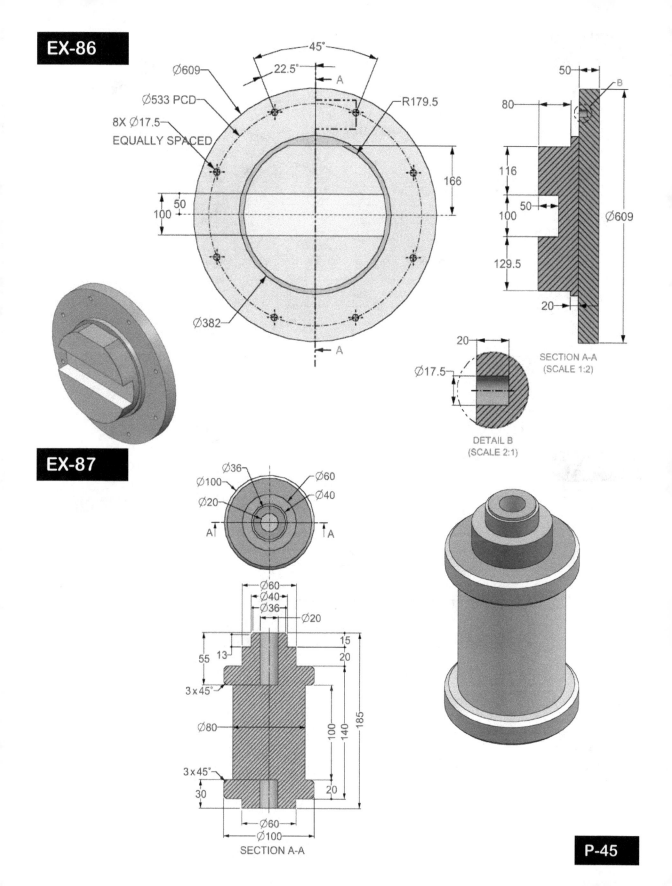

EX-86

Ø609
Ø533 PCD
8X Ø17.5
EQUALLY SPACED
Ø382
45°
22.5°
A
R179.5
166
50
100
50
80
116
50
100
129.5
20
Ø609
B
SECTION A-A
(SCALE 1:2)

20
Ø17.5
DETAIL B
(SCALE 2:1)

EX-87

Ø36
Ø100
Ø20
Ø60
Ø40
A
A
Ø60
Ø40
Ø36
Ø20
15
20
55
13
3 x 45°
Ø80
100
140
185
20
3 x 45°
30
Ø60
Ø100
SECTION A-A

P-45

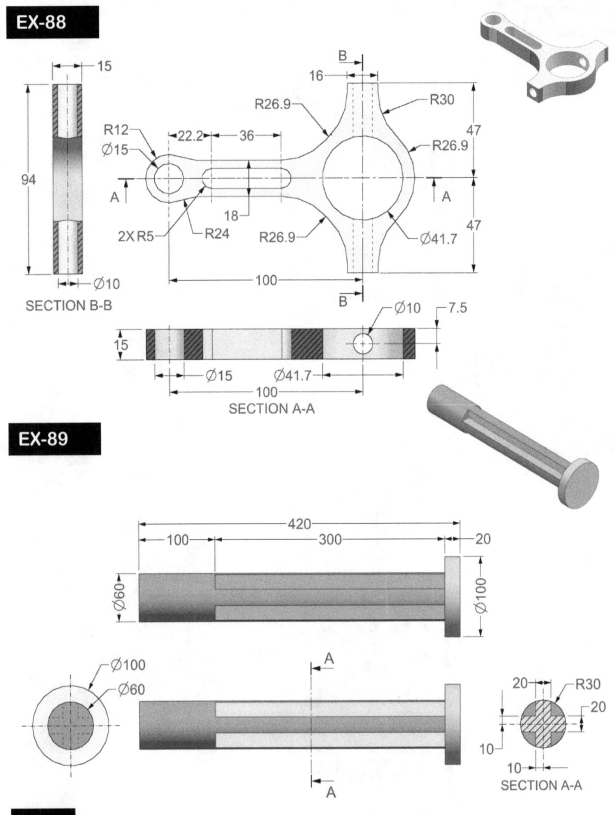

EX-88

15

94

Ø10

SECTION B-B

R12
Ø15

22.2

36

2X R5

R24

18

B

16

R26.9

R30

47

R26.9

47

R26.9

Ø41.7

100

B

Ø10

7.5

15

Ø15

Ø41.7

100

SECTION A-A

EX-89

420

100

300

20

Ø60

Ø100

Ø100

Ø60

A

A

20

R30

20

10

10

SECTION A-A

P-46

EX-90

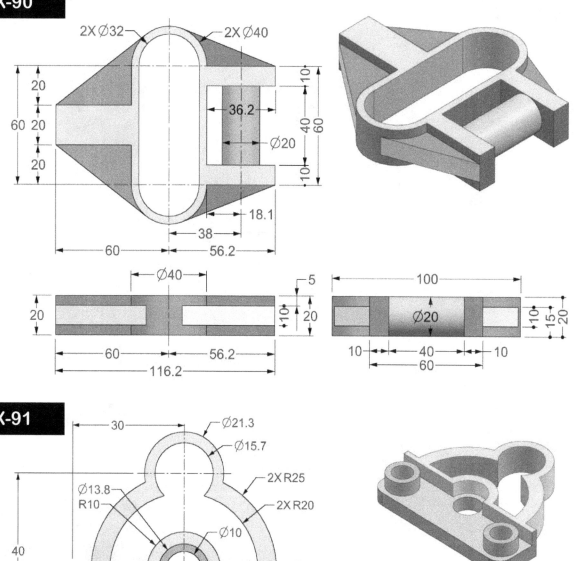

EX-91

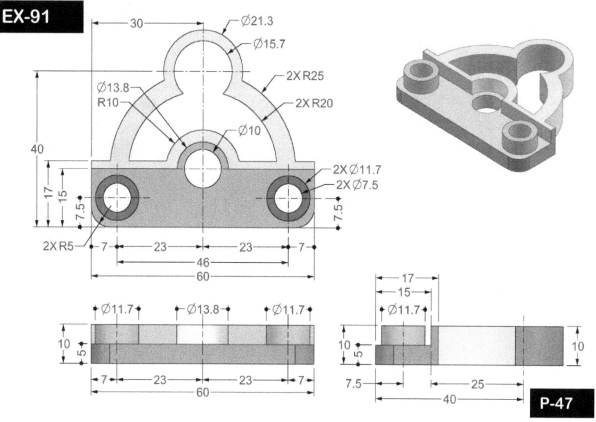

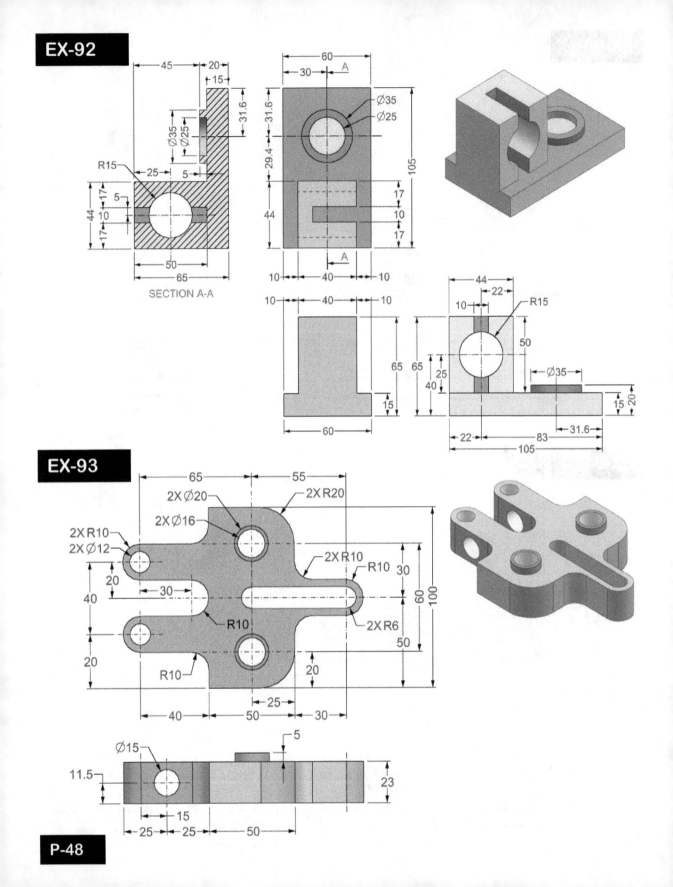

EX-92

SECTION A-A

EX-93

P-48

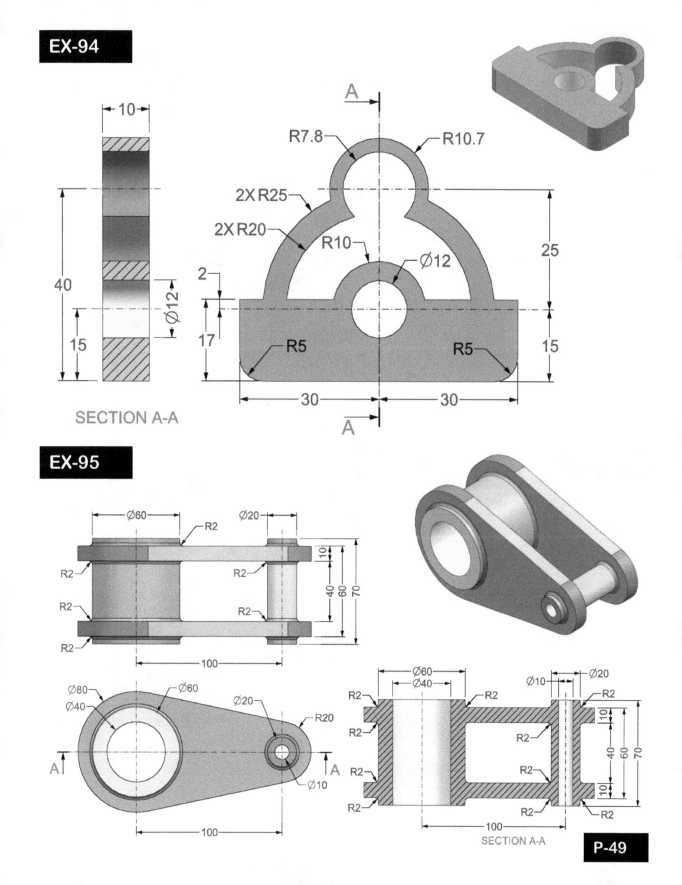

EX-94

10

40

15

Ø12

SECTION A-A

A

R7.8   R10.7

2X R25

2X R20

R10   Ø12

25

2

17

R5   R5

15

30   30

A

EX-95

Ø60   R2   Ø20

R2

R2   R2

R2   R2

10

40

60

70

100

Ø80   Ø60
Ø40   Ø20

R20

A   A

Ø10

100

Ø60   Ø20
Ø40

R2   R2   Ø10   R2

R2   R2

10

40

60

70

R2   R2

10

R2   R2

100

SECTION A-A

P-49

EX-96

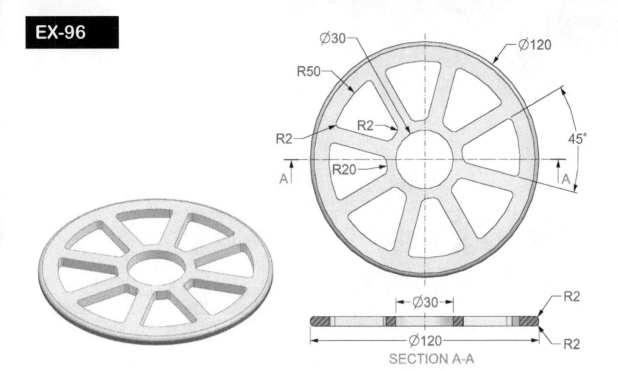

Ø30
R50
R2
R2
R20
Ø120
45°
Ø30
Ø120
R2
R2
SECTION A-A

EX-97

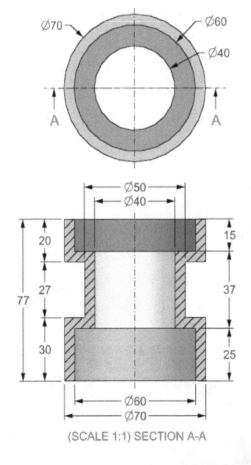
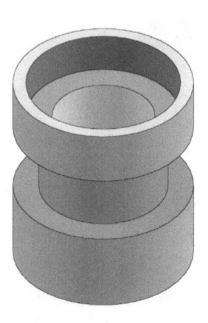

Ø70
Ø60
Ø40
A
A

Ø50
Ø40
20
15
77
27
37
30
25
Ø60
Ø70

(SCALE 1:1) SECTION A-A

P-50

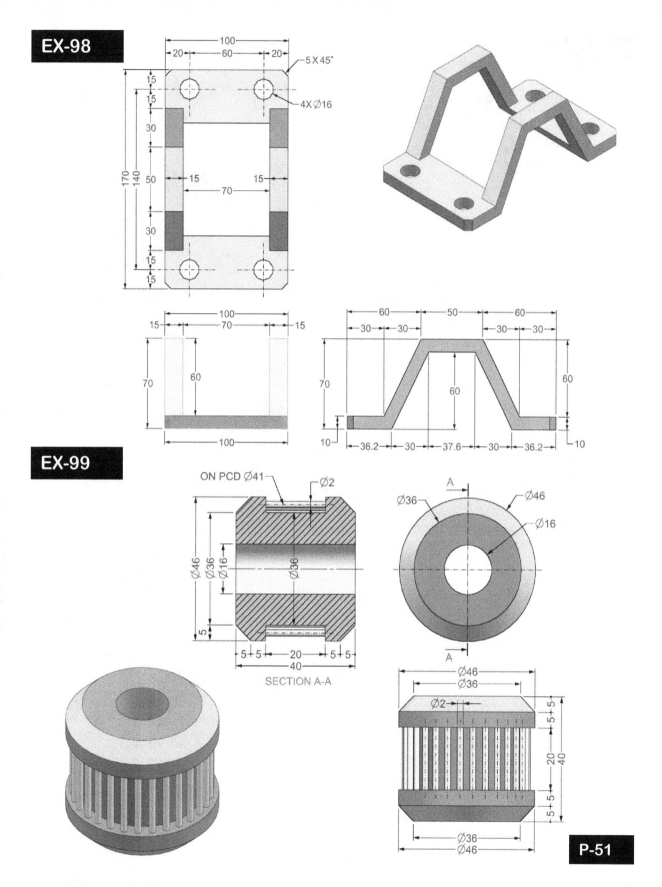

EX-98

EX-99

ON PCD Ø41   Ø2

Ø36   Ø46
Ø16

SECTION A-A

P-51

EX-100

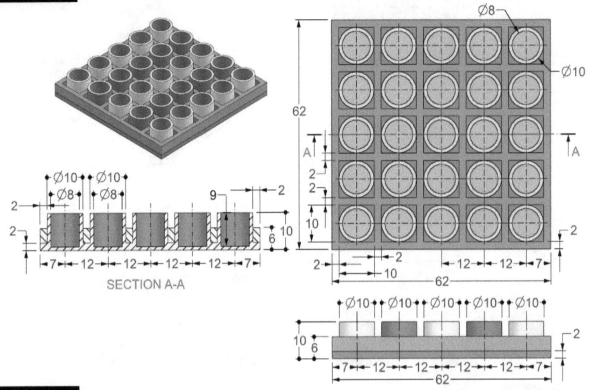

SECTION A-A

EX-101

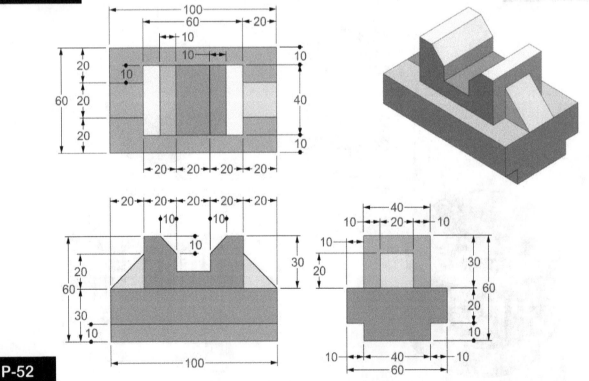

P-52

EX-102

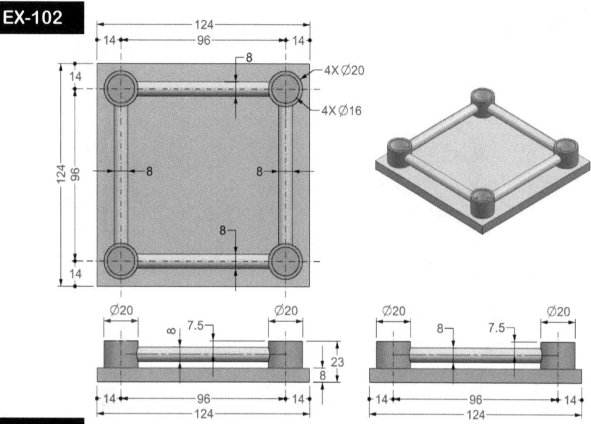

EX-103

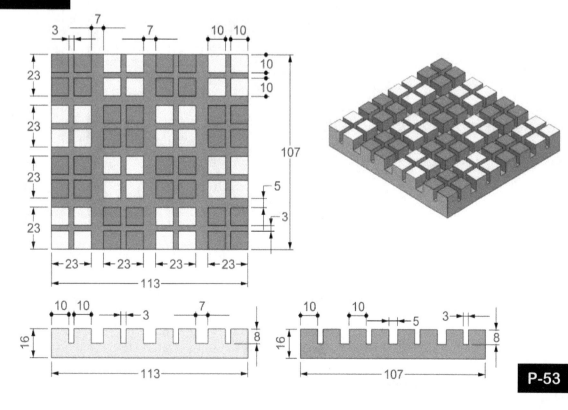

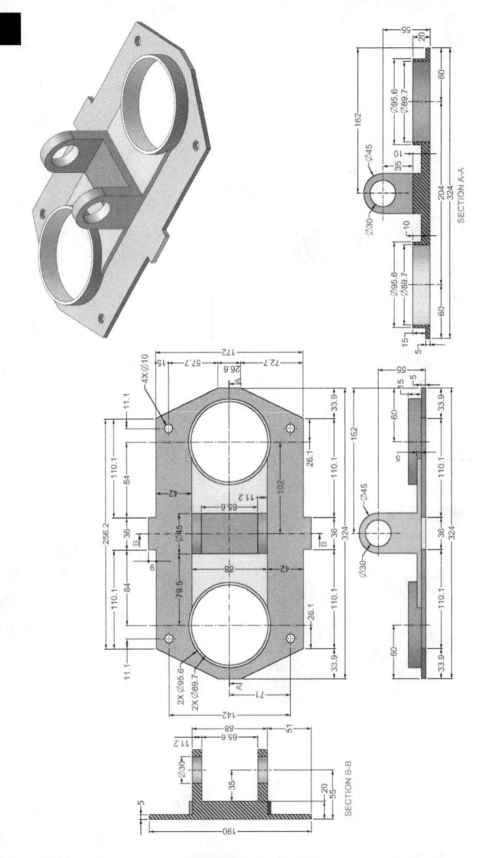

SECTION A-A

SECTION B-B

EX-105

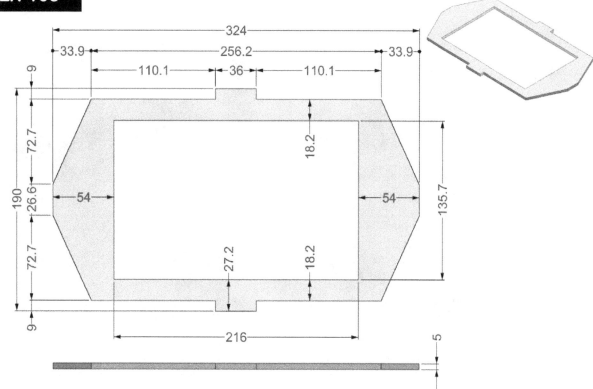

EX-106

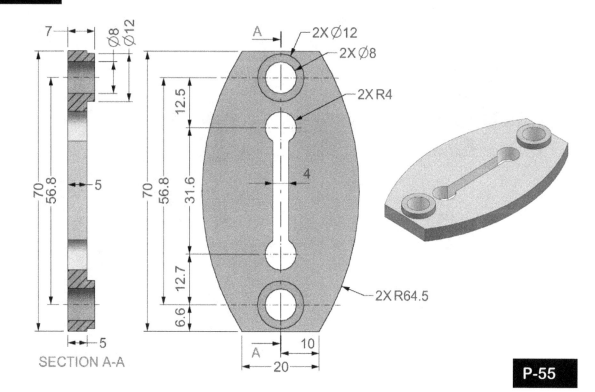

SECTION A-A

EX-107

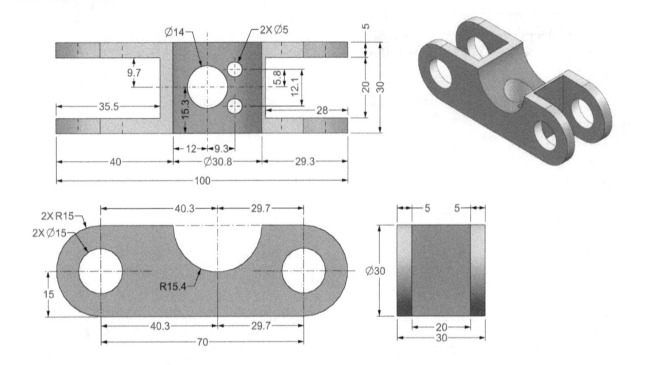

EX-108

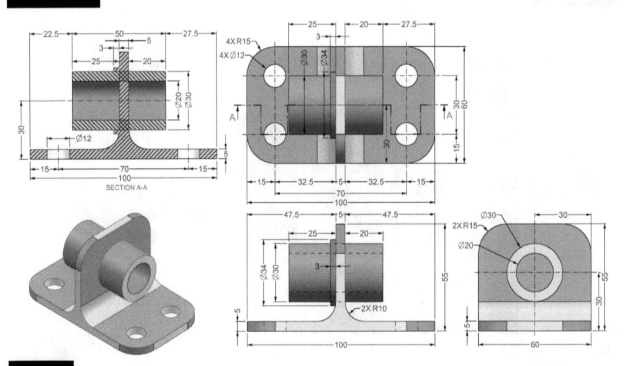

SECTION A-A

P-56

EX-109

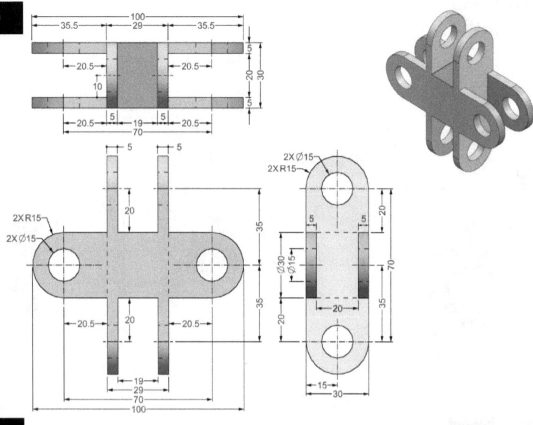

EX-110

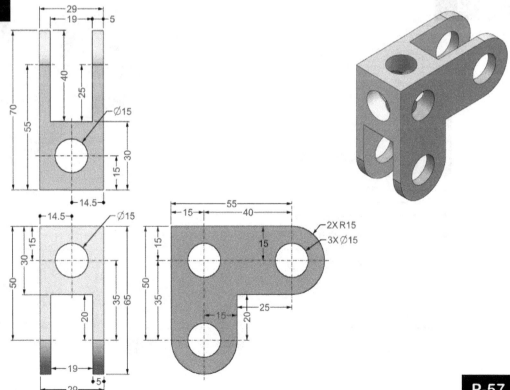

EX-111

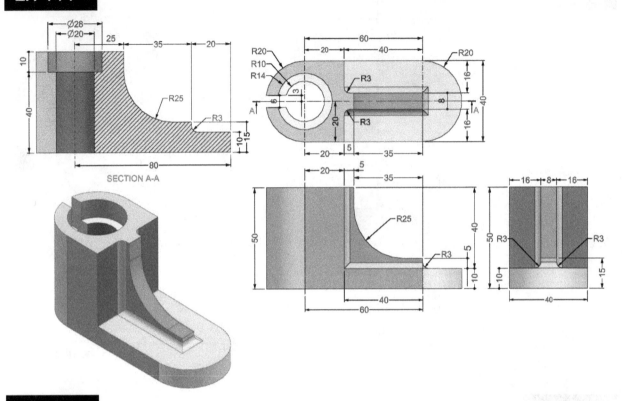

SECTION A-A

EX-112

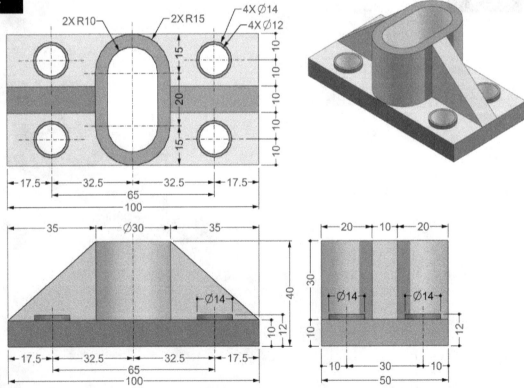

EX-113

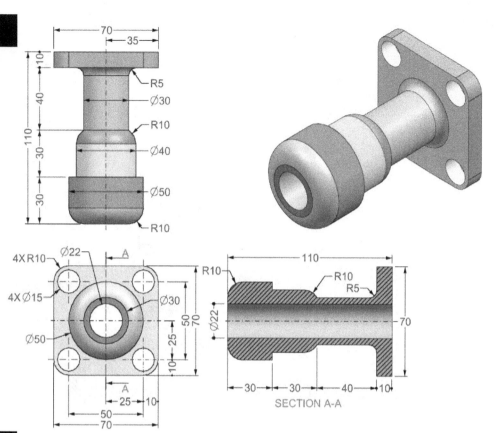

70
35
10
40
110
30
30

R5
Ø30
R10
Ø40
Ø50
R10

4X R10
Ø22
4X Ø15
Ø50
Ø30
50
70
25
10
A
A
25
10
50
70

R10
110
R10
R5
Ø22
70
30
30
40
10

SECTION A-A

EX-114

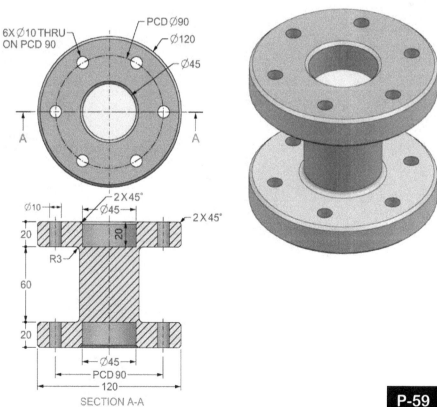

6X Ø10 THRU
ON PCD 90
PCD Ø90
Ø120
Ø45

A
A

Ø10
20
60
20
2 X 45°
Ø45
20
R3
2 X 45°
Ø45
PCD 90
120

SECTION A-A

P-59

EX-115

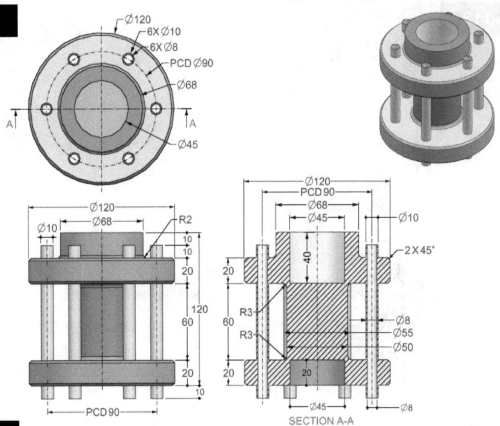

Ø120
6X Ø10
6X Ø8
PCD Ø90
Ø68
Ø45

A | A

Ø10
Ø120
Ø68
R2
10
10
20
120
60
20
10
PCD 90

Ø120
PCD 90
Ø68
Ø45
Ø10
40
2 X 45°
20
20
R3
60
R3
Ø8
Ø55
Ø50
20
20
20
Ø45
Ø8

SECTION A-A

EX-116

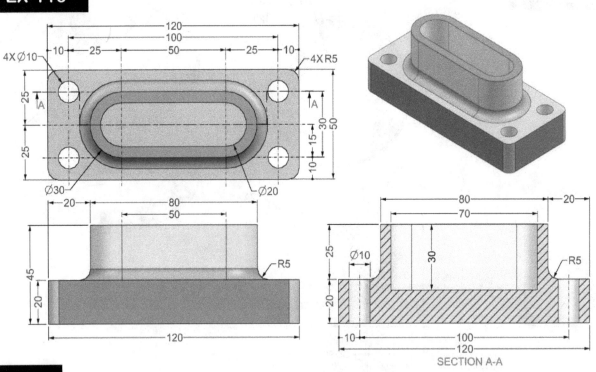

120
100
10
25
50
25
10
4X Ø10
4X R5
25
A
A
30
50
25
15
10
Ø30
Ø20

20
80
50
45
R5
20
120

80
20
70
25
Ø10
30
R5
20
10
100
120

SECTION A-A

P-60

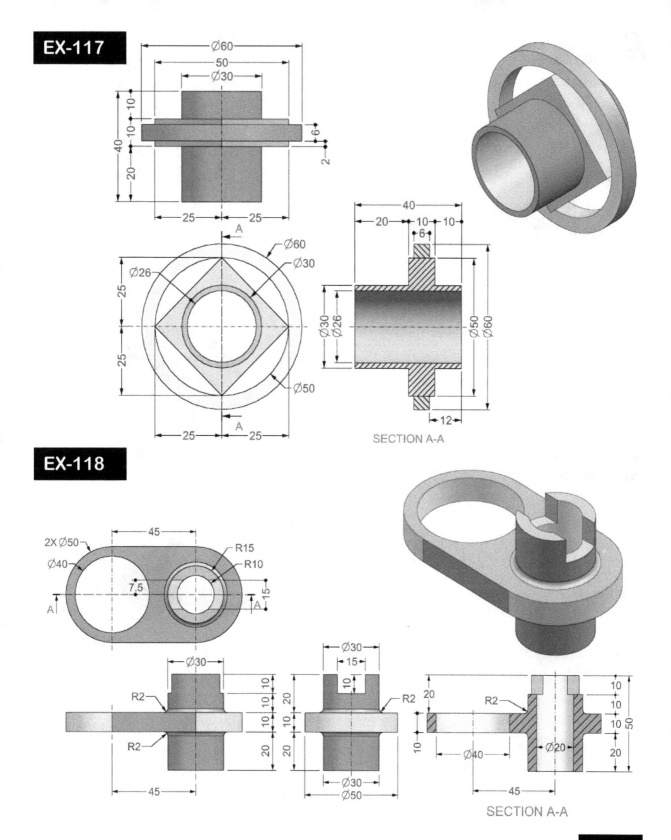

EX-117

EX-118

SECTION A-A

SECTION A-A

EX-119

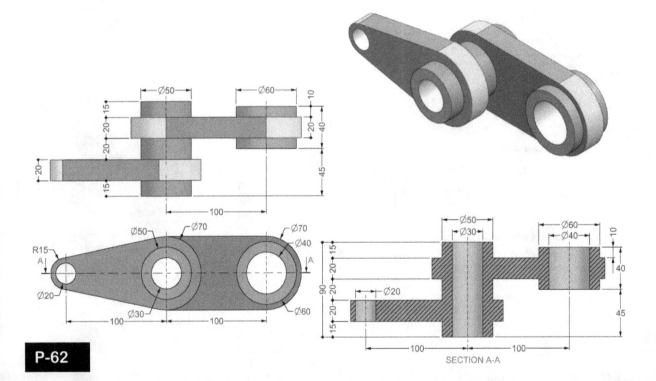

Ø190
Ø55

2X R20
2X R25
Ø140
70
25
50
Ø55
Ø75
Ø100
Ø180
Ø190
SECTION A-A

A
R25
25
50
A
Ø75
Ø190

Ø75
Ø55
Ø190
Ø180
Ø100

EX-120

Ø50
Ø60
10
15
20 20
20
40
20
45
20
15
100

R15
A
Ø50
Ø70
Ø70
Ø40
Ø20
Ø30
Ø60
100
100
A

Ø50
Ø30
Ø60
Ø40
10
20 15
20
20
90
Ø20
20
40
15 20
45
100
100
SECTION A-A

P-62

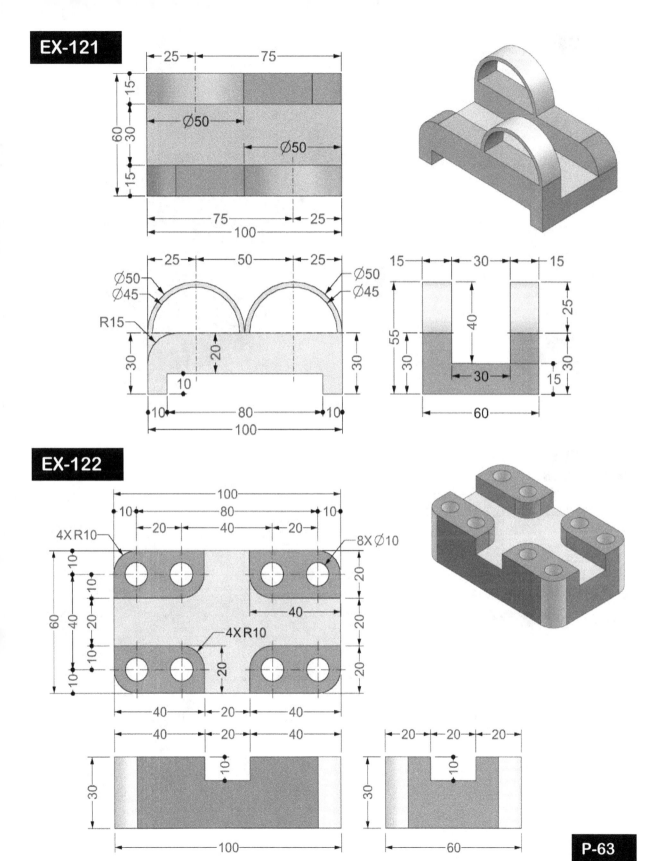

EX-121

EX-122

P-63

EX-123

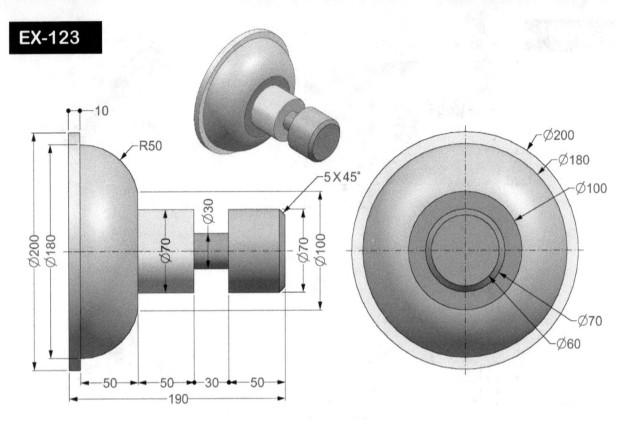

- 10
- R50
- 5 X 45°
- Ø30
- Ø70
- Ø70
- Ø100
- Ø200
- Ø180
- Ø200
- Ø180
- Ø100
- Ø70
- Ø60
- 50
- 50
- 30
- 50
- 190

EX-124

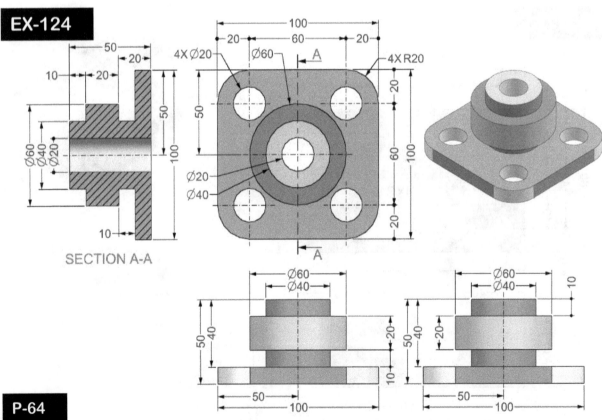

- 50
- 20
- 10
- 20
- Ø60
- Ø40
- Ø20
- 10
- SECTION A-A
- 100
- 20
- 60
- 20
- 4X Ø20
- Ø60
- A
- 4X R20
- 20
- 50
- 50
- 60
- 100
- Ø20
- Ø40
- 20
- A
- Ø60
- Ø40
- 50
- 40
- 50
- 100
- 20
- 10
- Ø60
- Ø40
- 10
- 50
- 40
- 20
- 50
- 100

P-64

EX-125

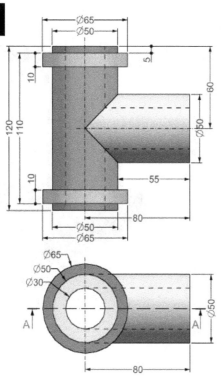

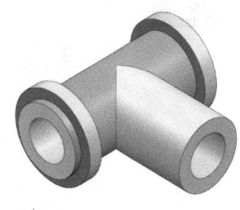

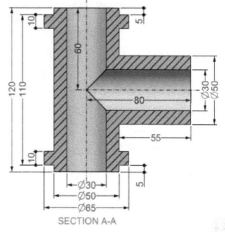

SECTION A-A

EX-126

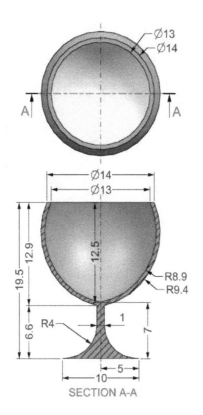

SECTION A-A

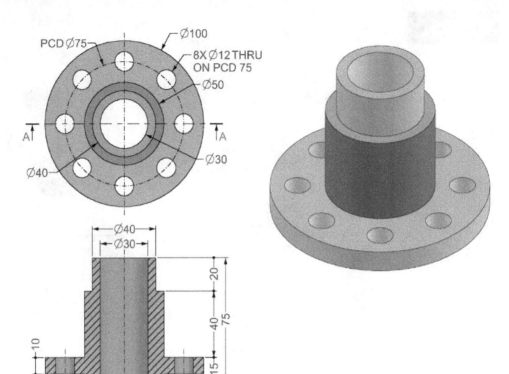

PCD Ø75
Ø100
8X Ø12 THRU
ON PCD 75
Ø50
A
A
Ø40
Ø30

Ø40
Ø30
20
75
40
10
15
Ø50
75
Ø100
SECTION A-A

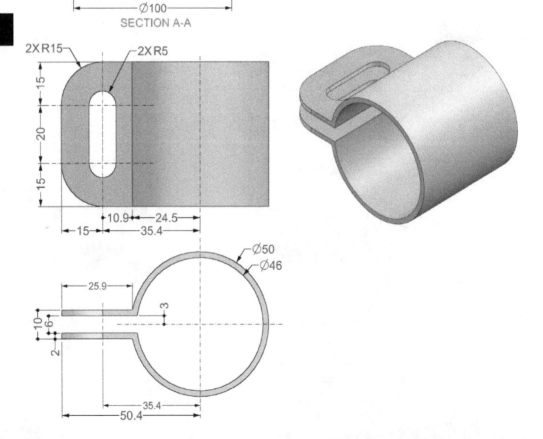

2X R15
2X R5
15
20
15
10.9
24.5
15
35.4

Ø50
Ø46
25.9
3
10
6
2
35.4
50.4

3X R20 3X Ø20 120°

R50

ØA A

Ø80

PCD Ø140

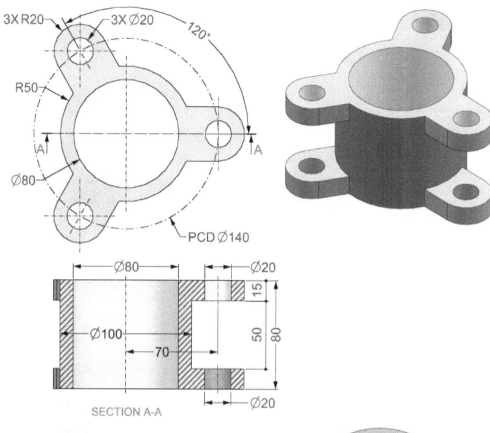

Ø80 Ø20

15

Ø100 50 80

70

Ø20

SECTION A-A

PCD Ø55 Ø70

A A

8X Ø8
ON PCD 55
Ø30 Ø40

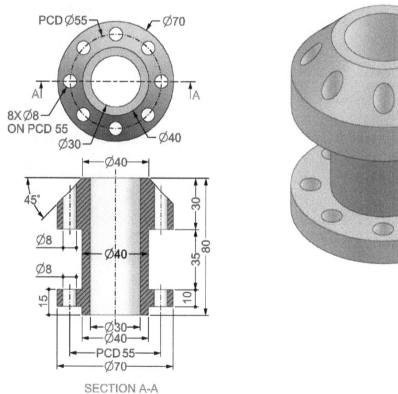

Ø40

45°

30

Ø8

Ø40 80

35

Ø8

10

15

Ø30
Ø40
PCD 55
Ø70

SECTION A-A

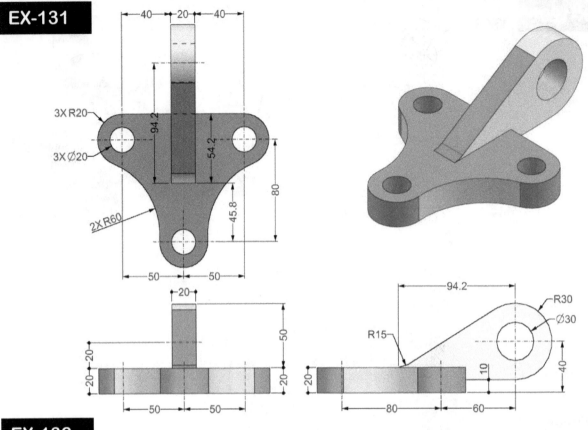

EX-132

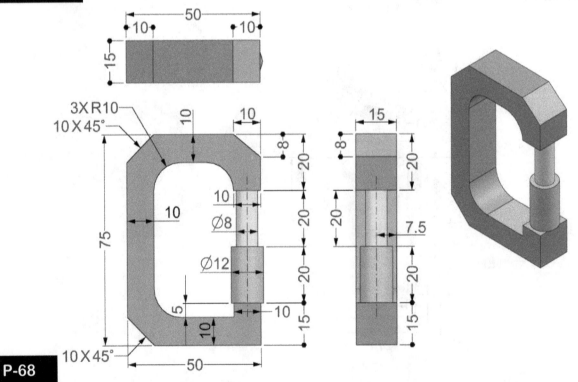

EX-133

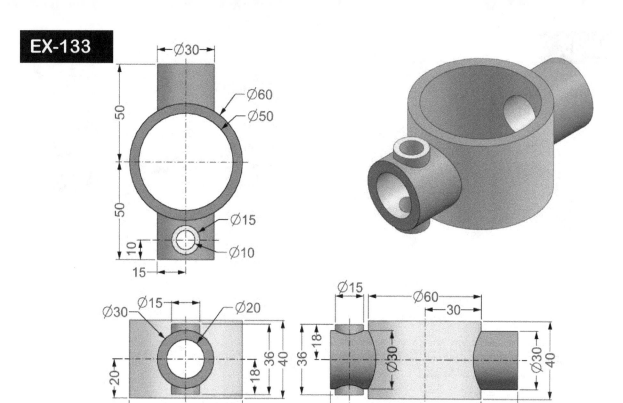

EX-134

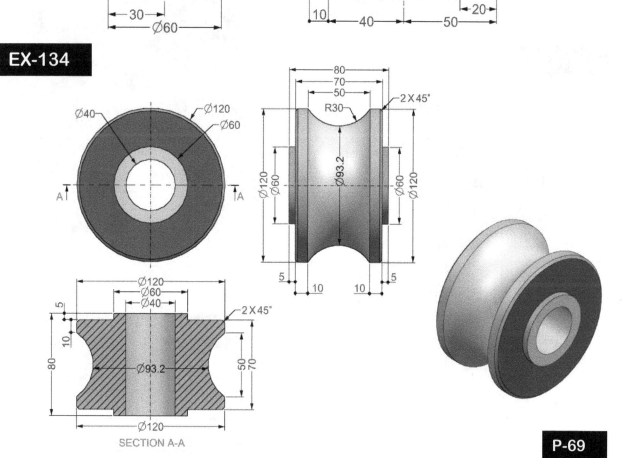

SECTION A-A

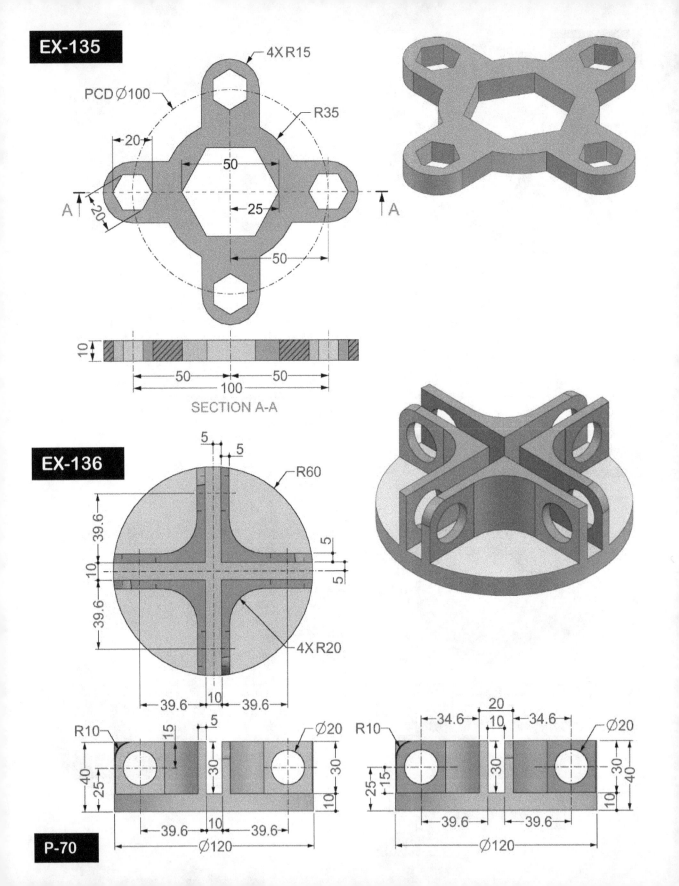

EX-135

4X R15
PCD ⌀100
R35
20
50
25
50
A
20°
A
10
50
50
100
SECTION A-A

EX-136

5
5
R60
39.6
39.6
10
39.6
4X R20
39.6
10
39.6

R10
15
5
⌀20
40
25
30
30
10
39.6
10
39.6
⌀120

R10
20
34.6
10
34.6
⌀20
25
15
30
30
40
10
39.6
39.6
10
⌀120

P-70

EX-137

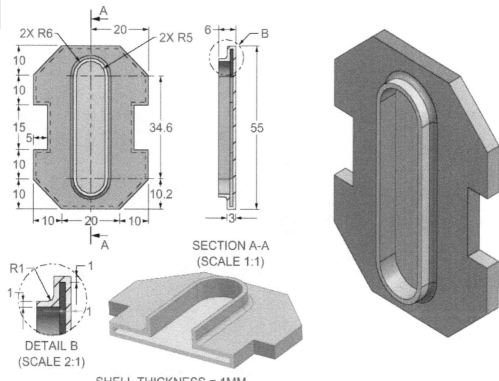

2X R6
2X R5

A
20
6
B

10
10
15
5
10
10
34.6
55
10.2

10
20
10
3

A

SECTION A-A
(SCALE 1:1)

R1
1
1
1
1

DETAIL B
(SCALE 2:1)

SHELL THICKNESS = 1MM
ALL INSIDE WALL THICKNESS

EX-138

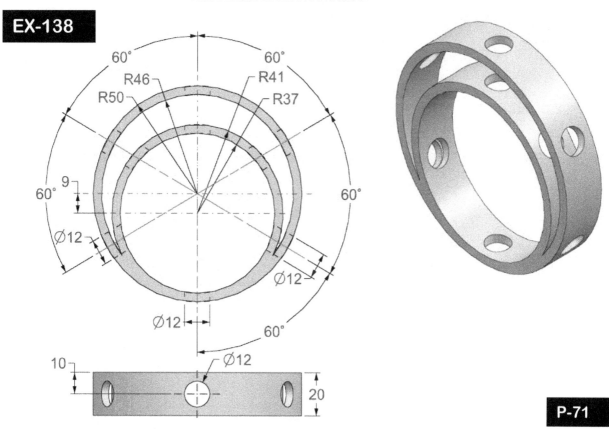

60°
60°
R46
R41
R50
R37
9
60°
60°
Ø12
Ø12
Ø12
60°
10
Ø12
20

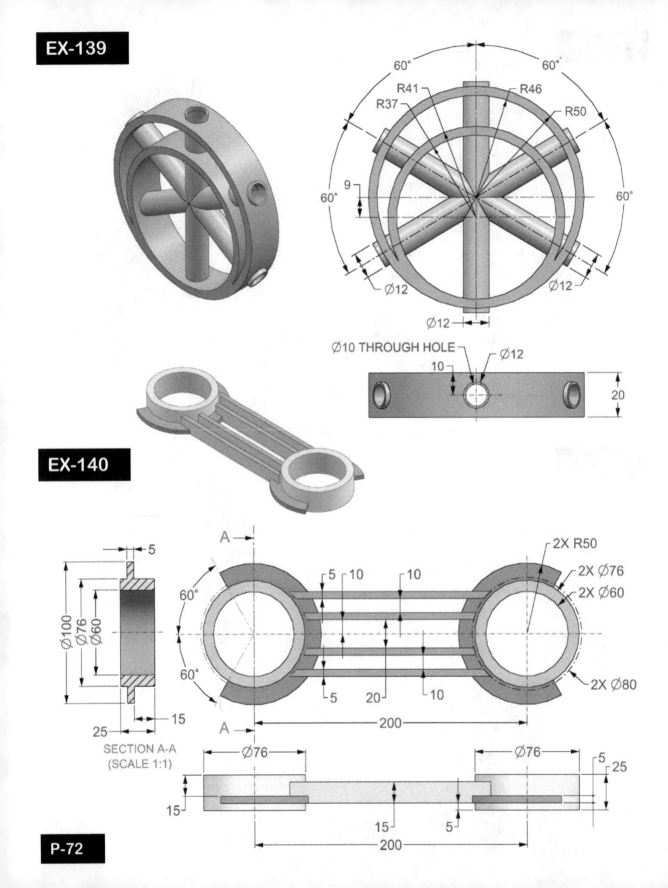

EX-139

60° 60°
R41 R46
R37 R50
60° 9
60° 60°
Ø12 Ø12
Ø12

Ø10 THROUGH HOLE Ø12
10
20

EX-140

A
2X R50
5 10 10 2X Ø76
60° 2X Ø60
Ø100 Ø76 Ø60 5
60° 5 20 10
5 10 2X Ø80
15 A 200
25 SECTION A-A
(SCALE 1:1)

Ø76 Ø76 5
25
15 15 5
200

P-72

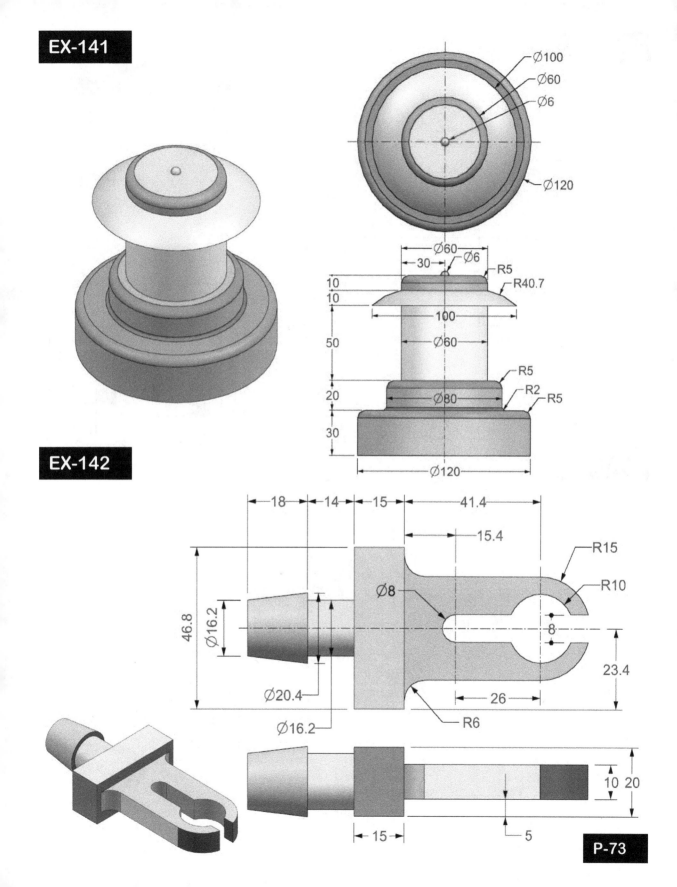

EX-141

Ø100
Ø60
Ø6
Ø120

Ø60
30
Ø6
R5
10
10
R40.7
100
50
Ø60
20
R5
Ø80
R2 R5
30
Ø120

EX-142

18
14
15
41.4
15.4
R15
R10
46.8
Ø16.2
Ø8
8
23.4
Ø20.4
26
R6
Ø16.2

10 20
15
5

P-73

EX-143

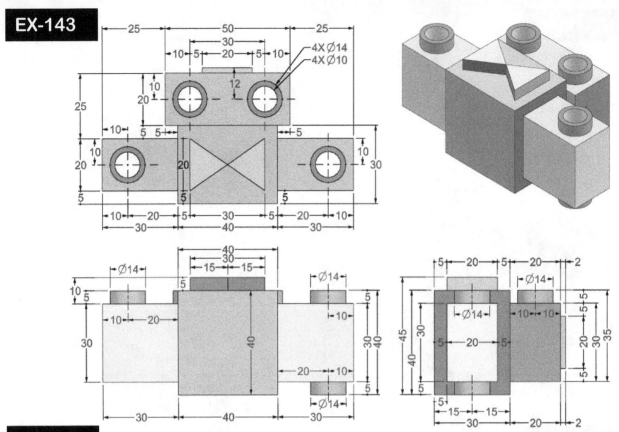

EX-144

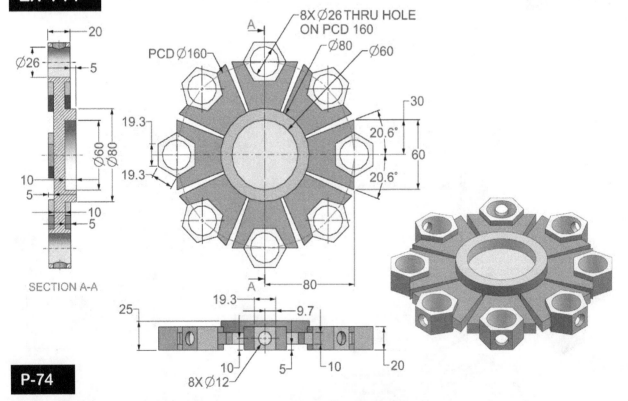

SECTION A-A

8X Ø26 THRU HOLE
ON PCD 160

PCD Ø160

Ø80

Ø60

8X Ø12

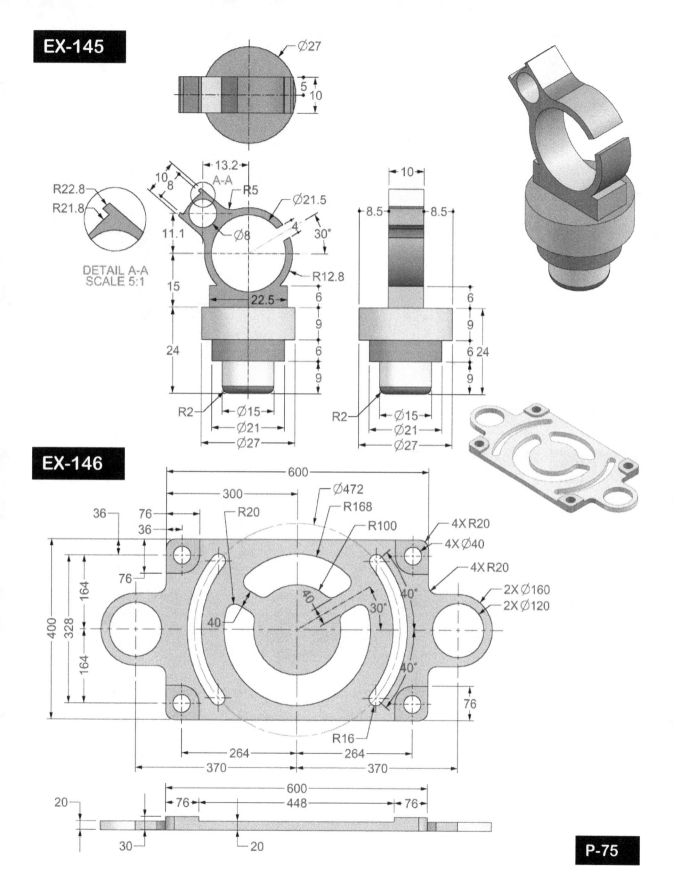

EX-145

Ø27
5
10

13.2
10
8
A-A
R5
Ø21.5
R22.8
R21.8
Ø8
4
30°
11.1
DETAIL A-A
SCALE 5:1
R12.8
15
22.5
6
9
24
6
9
R2
Ø15
Ø21
Ø27

10
8.5
8.5
6
9
6 24
9
R2
Ø15
Ø21
Ø27

EX-146

600
300
Ø472
R168
R100
R20
4X R20
4X Ø40
36
76
36
4X R20
76
2X Ø160
2X Ø120
164
40
40°
400
328
30°
40
164
40°
76
R16
264
264
370
370

600
448
20
76
76
76
30
20

P-75

Ø40
120°
Ø20
120°
10
60

R10
Ø40
200
79.6
Ø20
15
60
R15

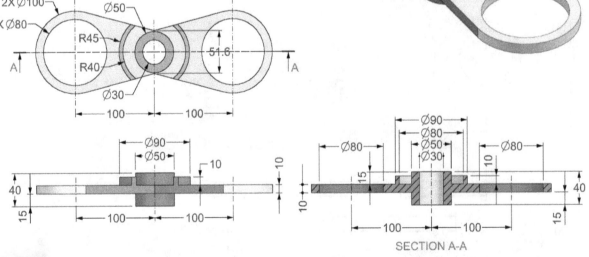

2X Ø100
2X Ø80
Ø50
R45
51.6
A
R40
Ø30
100
100

Ø90
Ø50
10
10
40
15
100
100

Ø90
Ø80
Ø50
Ø30
Ø80
Ø80
15
10
10
40
15
100
100

SECTION A-A

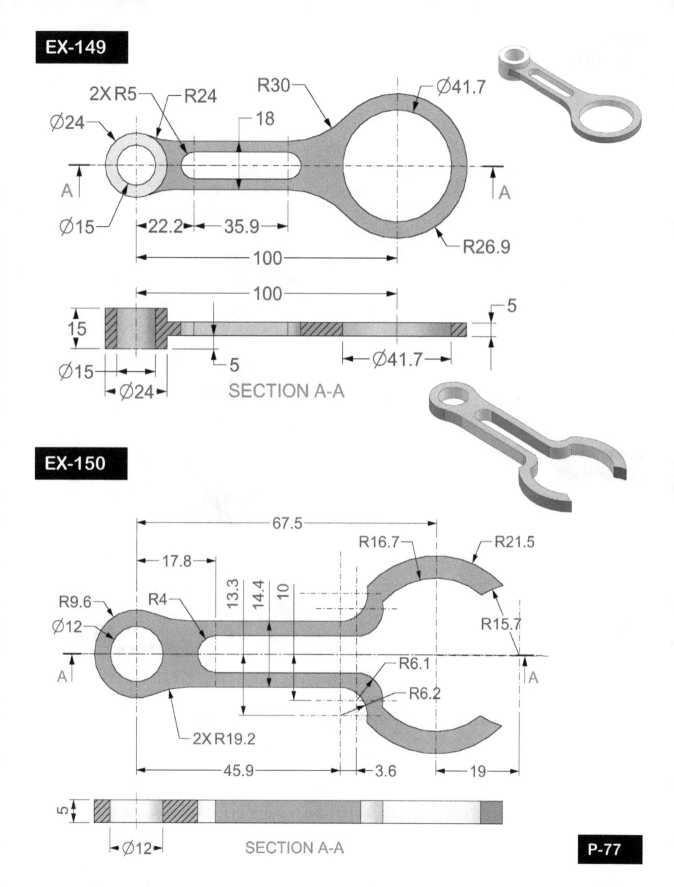

EX-149

2X R5 — R24 R30 ∅41.7

∅24

18

R26.9

∅15

2X R5

22.2 35.9

100

100

5

15

∅15

∅24

5

∅41.7

SECTION A-A

EX-150

67.5

17.8

R16.7 R21.5

13.3 14.4 10

R9.6 R4

∅12

R15.7

A

R6.1

R6.2

2X R19.2

45.9 3.6 19

5

∅12

SECTION A-A

P-77

Ø8
6.5
R1.5
10
R1.5
28
1:1
B-B
27
Ø10
SECTION A-A

Ø20
A
R3
35
15°
20
5
A
Ø13.3
Ø16

R8
R10
R6.7
R4
R5

1
45°
DETAIL B-B
SCALE 5:1

Ø20
Ø36
Ø58
Ø52
Ø16

Ø36
Ø20
R8
8
20
2
135°
13.5
Ø16
R11.2
76
15.8
21.6
10.7
13
10
R6
Ø16
R3
SECTION A-A

A
58
3
R3
R2
Ø52
76
R6
A
40

EX-153

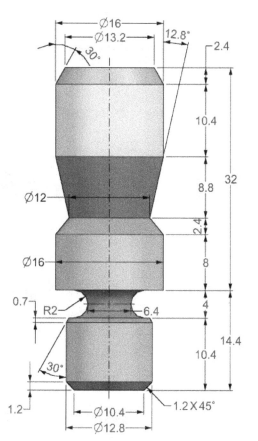

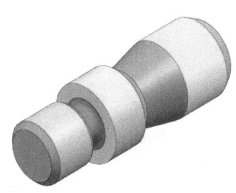

Ø16
Ø13.2
12.8°
30°
2.4
10.4
32
8.8
Ø12
2.4
Ø16
8
0.7
R2
6.4
4
14.4
10.4
30°
1.2
Ø10.4
1.2 X 45°
Ø12.8

EX-154

Ø40
Ø12
Ø4.5

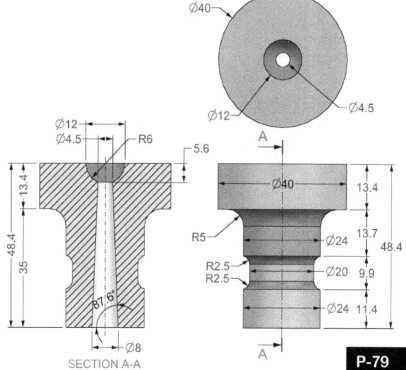

Ø12
Ø4.5
R6
5.6
A
Ø40
13.4
48.4
35
13.7
Ø24
R5
R2.5
Ø20
R2.5
9.9
Ø24
11.4
87.6°
Ø8
A
SECTION A-A

P-79

EX-155

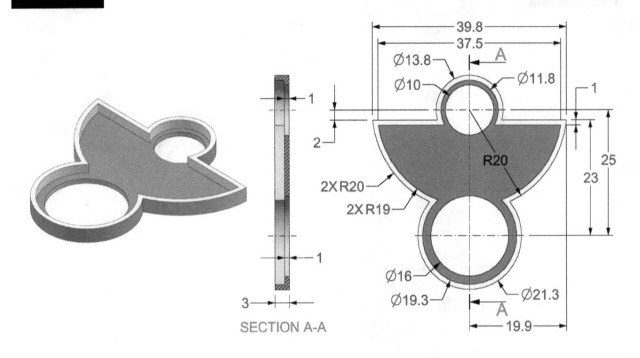

Ø13.8
Ø10
Ø11.8
39.8
37.5
A
1
2
R20
25
23
2X R20
2X R19
Ø16
Ø19.3
Ø21.3
A
19.9

SECTION A-A

1
3
1

EX-156

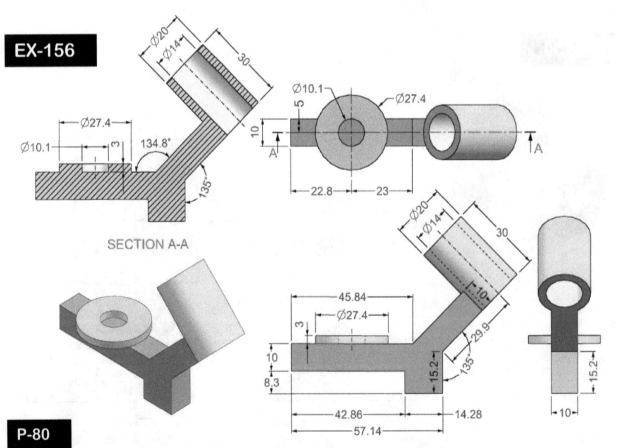

Ø20
Ø14
30
Ø27.4
Ø10.1
3
134.8°
135°

SECTION A-A

Ø10.1
5
Ø27.4
10
A
22.8
23
A

Ø20
Ø14
30
10
Ø27.4
3
29.9
135°
15.2
45.84
10
8.3
42.86
14.28
57.14
15.2
10

P-80

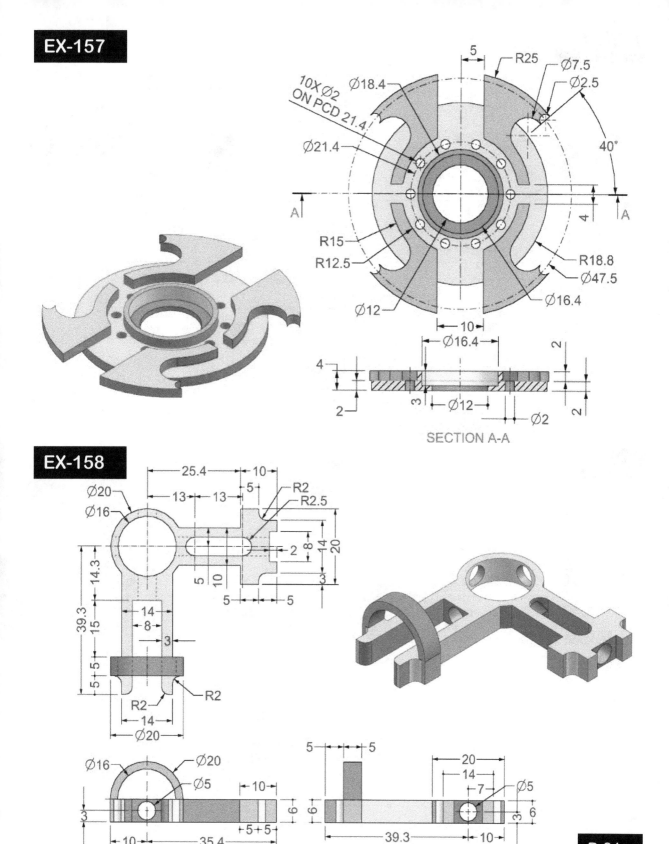

EX-157

10X Ø2
ON PCD 21.4

Ø18.4
Ø21.4
5
R25
Ø7.5
Ø2.5
40°
R15
R12.5
Ø12
Ø16.4
R18.8
Ø47.5
A
A
4
10

Ø16.4
4
2
2
3
Ø12
Ø2
2

SECTION A-A

EX-158

25.4
10
13
13
5
R2
R2.5
Ø20
Ø16
2
8
14
20
5
10
3
14.3
14
8
5
5
39.3
15
3
5
5
R2
R2

14
Ø20

Ø16
Ø20
Ø5
3
10
10
35.4
5 5
6

5
5
20
14
7
Ø5
6
6
3
6
39.3
10

P-81

EX-159

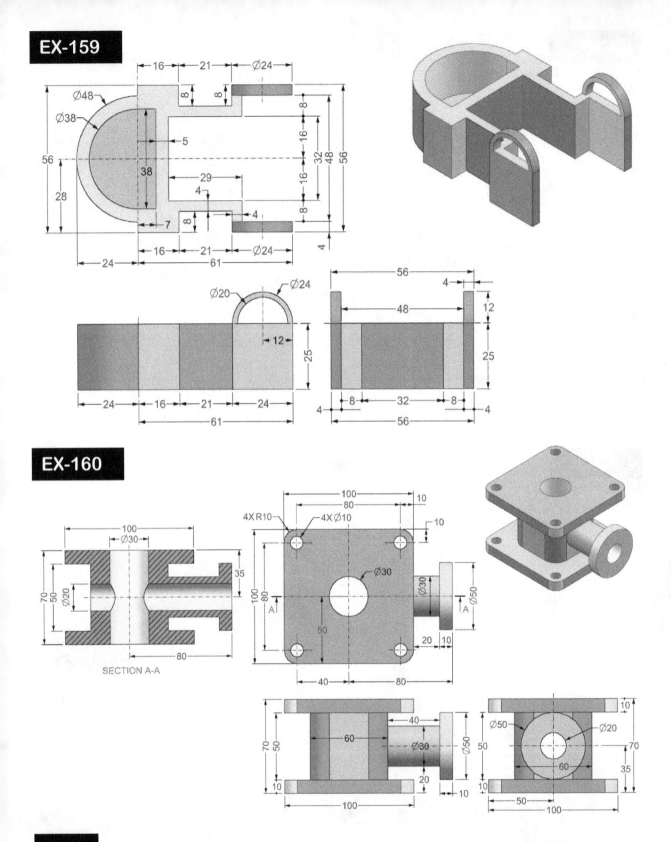

EX-160

SECTION A-A

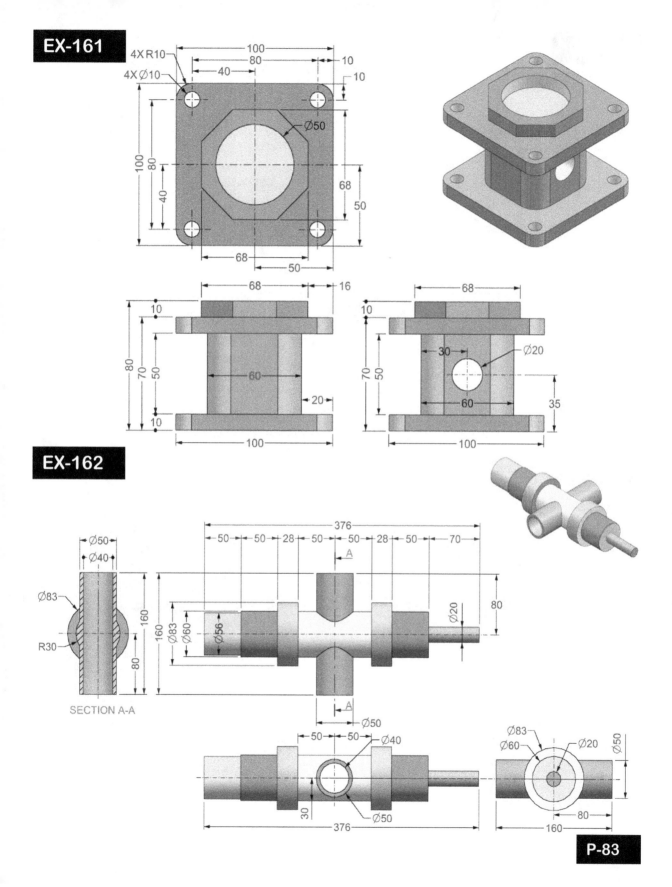

EX-161

EX-162

SECTION A-A

P-83

EX-163

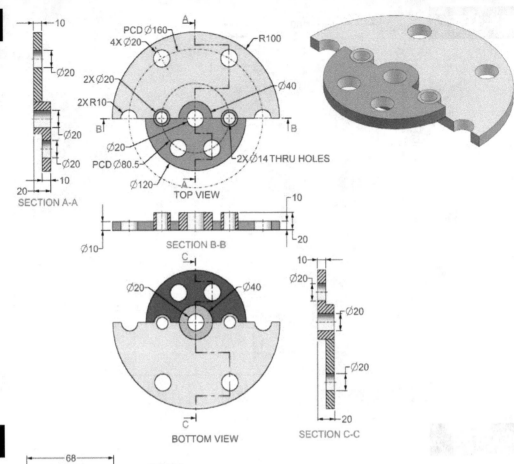

SECTION A-A

10
Ø20
Ø20
Ø20
20 — 10

TOP VIEW

PCD Ø160
4X Ø20
2X Ø20
2X R10
PCD Ø80.5
Ø120
R100
Ø40
2X Ø14 THRU HOLES
Ø20

SECTION B-B

10
20
Ø10

BOTTOM VIEW

Ø20
Ø40
Ø20

SECTION C-C

10
Ø20
Ø20
Ø20
20

EX-164

68
28.2
4X R10
4X Ø10
10
Ø50
Ø30
68
28.2
A
A
80
100
40
10
10 — 40 — 40 — 10
80
100

16 — 68 — 16
28.2
10 10
80
70
50
Ø18
25
30
60
10
35
50
100

100
68
Ø50
10 10
10
50
Ø18
25
Ø30
50 — 50
100
SECTION A-A

P-84

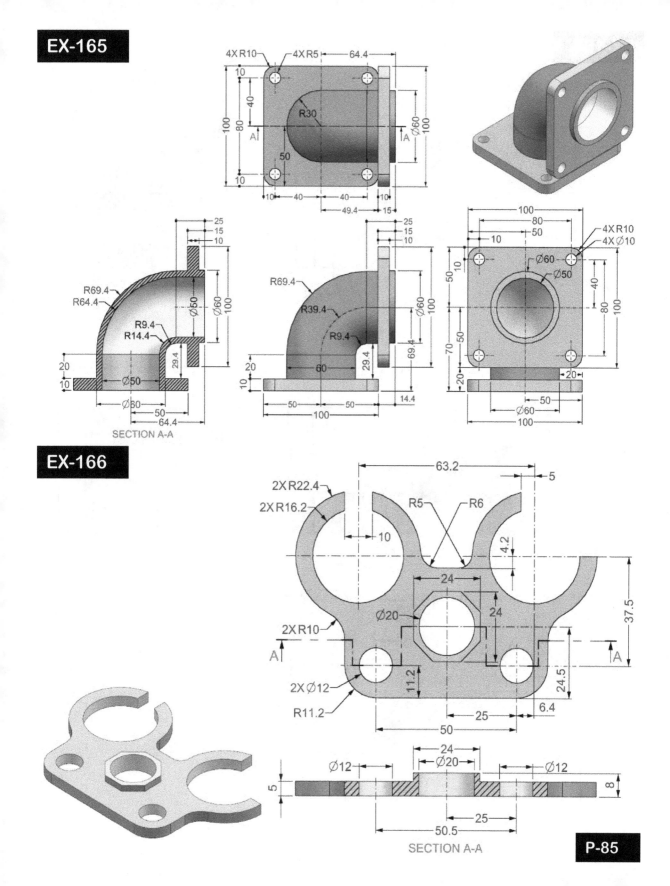

EX-165

4X R10   4X R5   64.4
10
40
80
100
R30
Ai   A
50
10
10   40   40   10
49.4   15
Ø60
100

25
15
10
R69.4
R64.4
R9.4
R14.4
Ø50
Ø60
100
20
10
29.4
Ø50
Ø60
50
64.4
SECTION A-A

25
15
10
R69.4
R39.4
R9.4
Ø60
100
69.4
20
10
60
29.4
50   50
100
14.4

100
80
50
10
4X R10
4X Ø10
Ø60
Ø50
50
10
40
80
100
50
70
20
20
50
Ø60
100

EX-166

63.2   5
2X R22.4
2X R16.2
R5   R6
10
4.2
24
Ø20
24
37.5
2X R10
A
11.2
24.5
2X Ø12
R11.2
6.4
25
50

24
Ø12   Ø20   Ø12
5
8
25
50.5
SECTION A-A

P-85

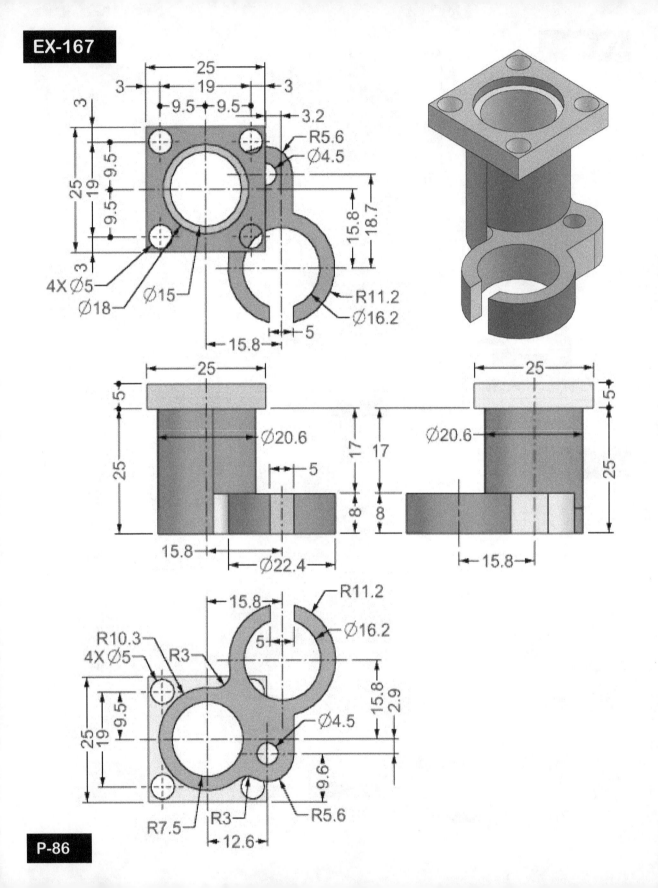

EX-168

PCD Ø95
Ø120
8X Ø14
8X Ø10
ON PCD 95
R35
R25
6
3

A

A

32
30
80 16
32
20
2
Ø70
Ø120

30
Ø14
Ø10
16 20
Ø50
Ø70
PCD 95
Ø120

SECTION A-A

EX-169

Ø70
Ø40
20
R5
40
Ø28
Ø40
50
130
70
200

Ø70
R2
R60
30
Ø80
21.3
40
50
R5
140
80
Ø28
Ø40
30
10
50
80
70

Ø70
15
40
15
10
30
Ø28
Ø40
80
15
15
70
30
10
35
Ø70

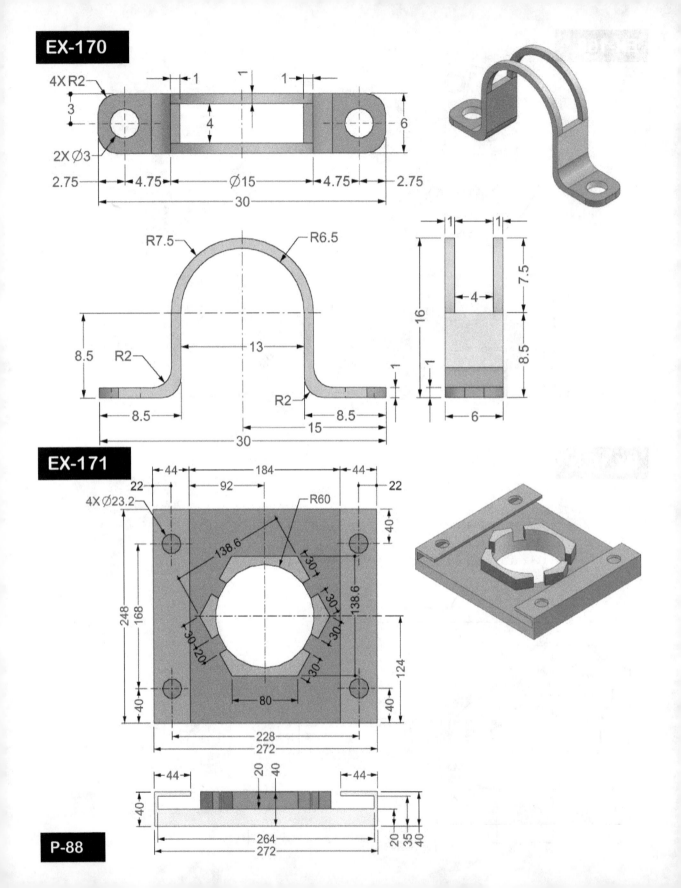

EX-170

4X R2

3

2X Ø3

2.75 — 4.75 — Ø15 — 4.75 — 2.75

30

1

1

4

6

R7.5   R6.5

R2

8.5

13

8.5   R2

8.5   15   8.5

30

1   1

16   7.5

4

1   8.5

6

EX-171

44   184   44

22   92   22

4X Ø23.2   R60

138.6   30

30

30

30-20

30

248   168   138.6

124

80   40

40

228

272

44   20   40   44

40   264   20 35 40

272

P-88

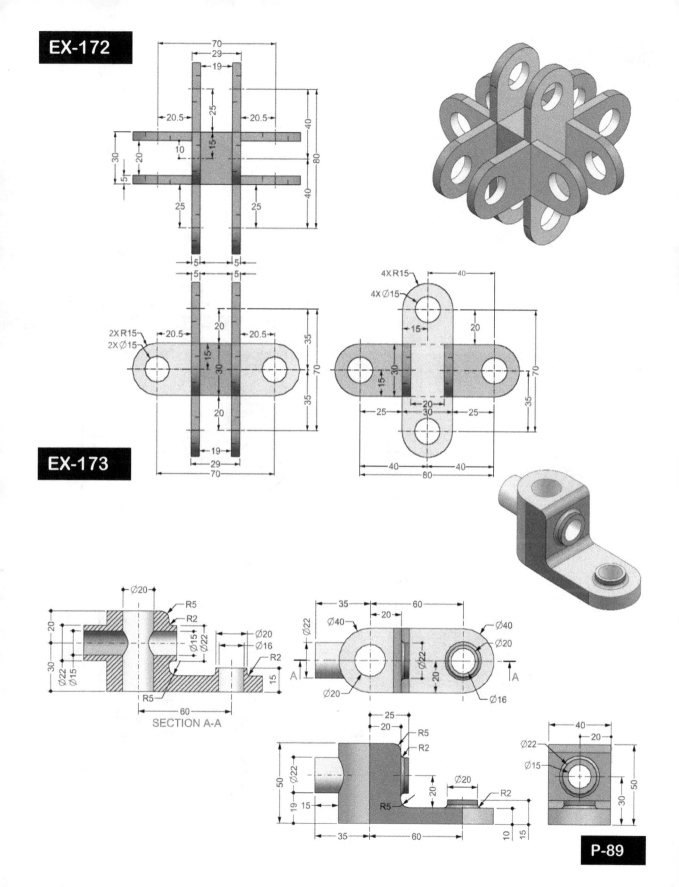

EX-172

EX-173

2X R15
2X Ø15

4X R15
4X Ø15

SECTION A-A

P-89

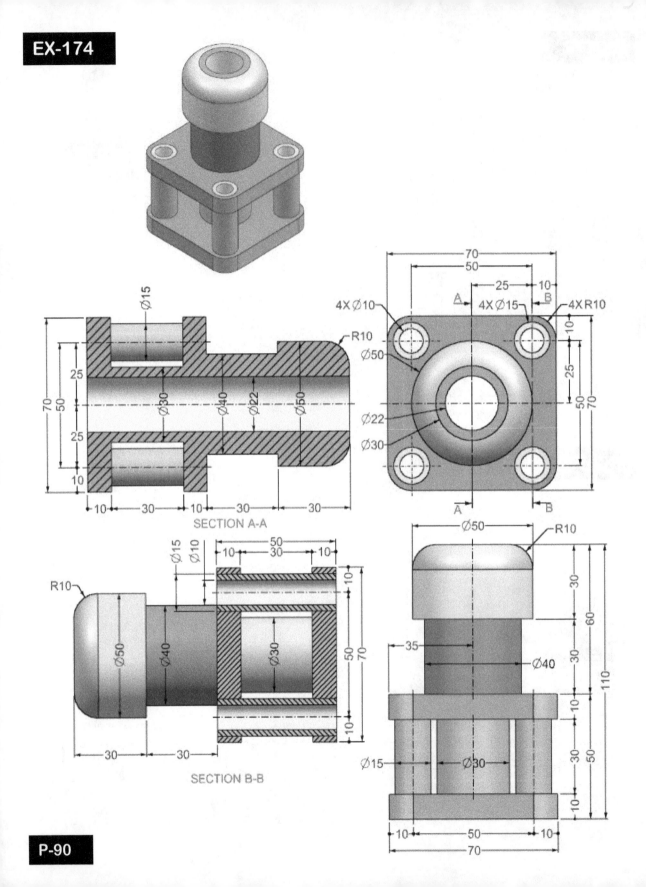

SECTION A-A

SECTION B-B

4X Ø10

4X Ø15

4X R10

4X Ø15
4X Ø10
Ø30
Ø22
4X R10

70
35 35
10 25 25 10

10
35
25
70
25
35
10

A A

Ø30
Ø15 Ø15
Ø15 Ø15
50
70

20
5
10
30
50
10

SECTION A-A

Ø30
Ø22
Ø15
Ø10
20
Ø22

25 25
50
70

5
10
30
70
30
10

EX-176

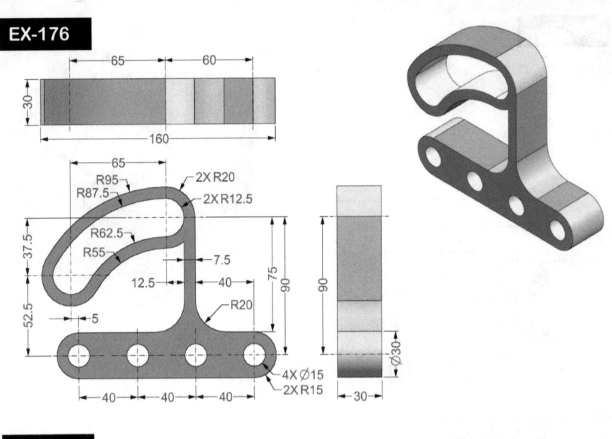

EX-177

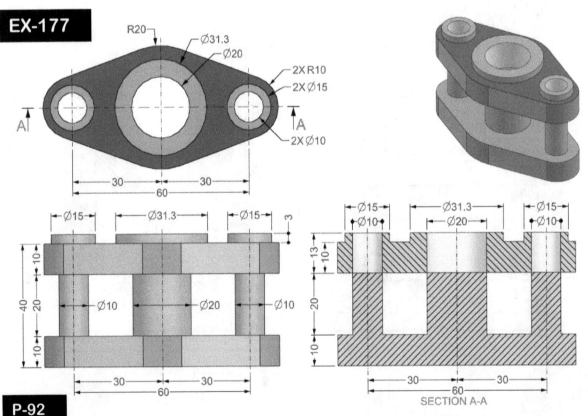

SECTION A-A

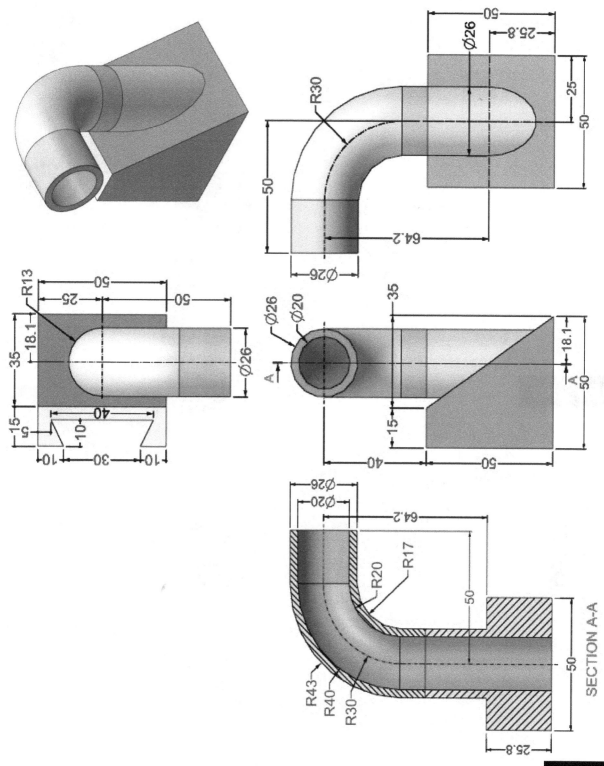

SECTION A-A

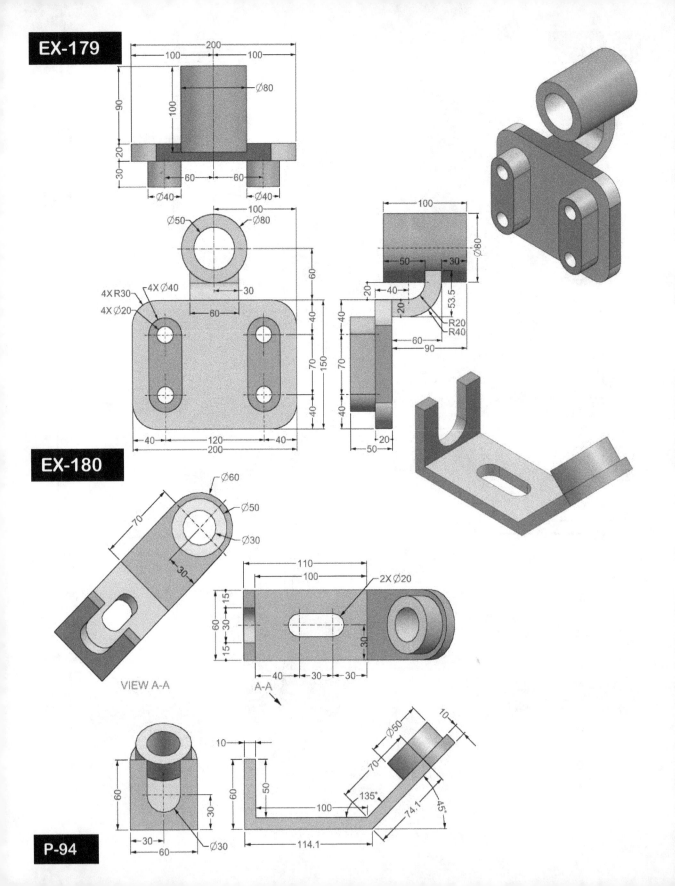

EX-179

Ø80

200
100 100
90
100
Ø80
20
30
60 60
Ø40 Ø40

Ø50 Ø80
100
4X R30 4X Ø40
4X Ø20 30
60
40
70 150
60
40
40 120 40
200

100
50 30
20
40 Ø80
20 53.5
R20
R40
60
90
40
70
40
20
50

EX-180

Ø60
Ø50
70
Ø30
30

VIEW A-A

110
100
2X Ø20
15
60 30
15 30
40 30 30
A-A

P-94

Ø50 10
70
60
30
135°
60 50
100
10
45°
74.1
30 Ø30
60 114.1

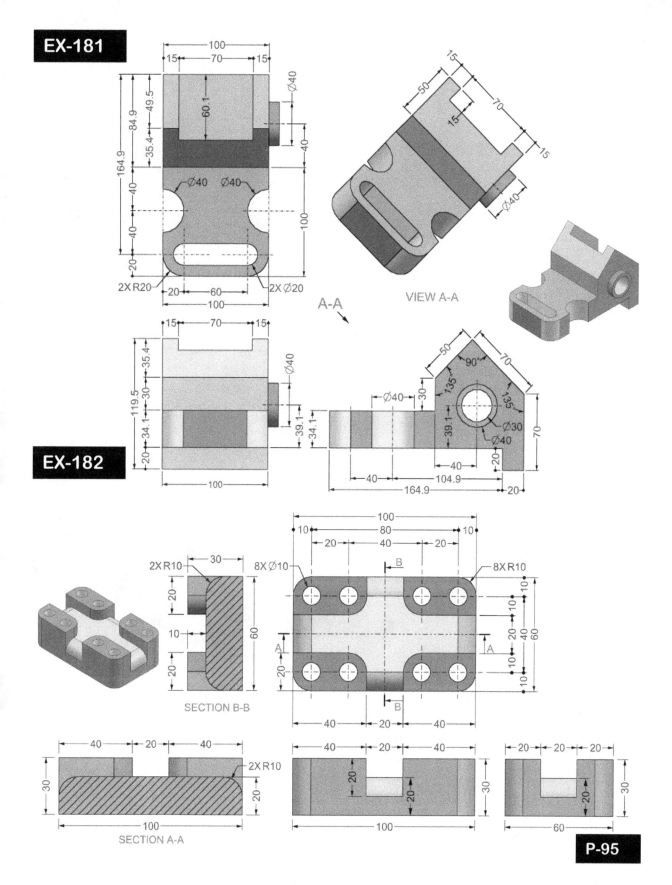

EX-181

EX-182

VIEW A-A

A-A

SECTION B-B

SECTION A-A

P-95

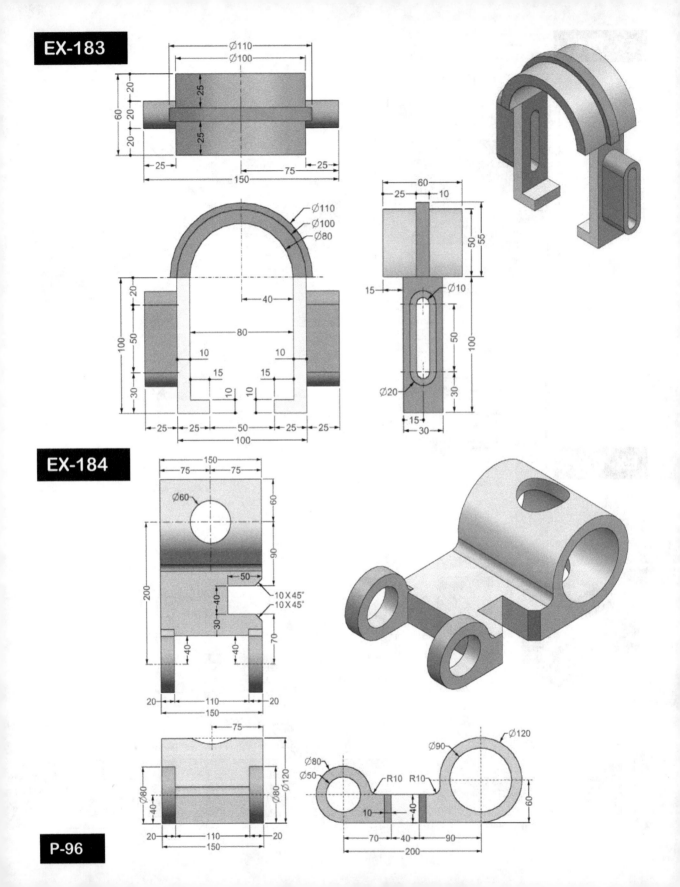

EX-183

Ø110
Ø100
20
20
60
25
20
25
25
75
25
150

Ø110
Ø100
Ø80
20
100
50
40
80
30
10
10
15
15
10
10
25 25 50 25 25
100

60
25 10
50
55
15
Ø10
50
100
Ø20
30
15
30

EX-184

150
75 75
Ø60
60
90
200
50
40
10 X 45°
40
30
10 X 45°
70
40
40
20 110 20
150

75
Ø80
40
Ø80
Ø120
20 110 20
150

Ø80
Ø50
Ø90
Ø120
R10 R10
10
40
60
70 40 90
200

P-96

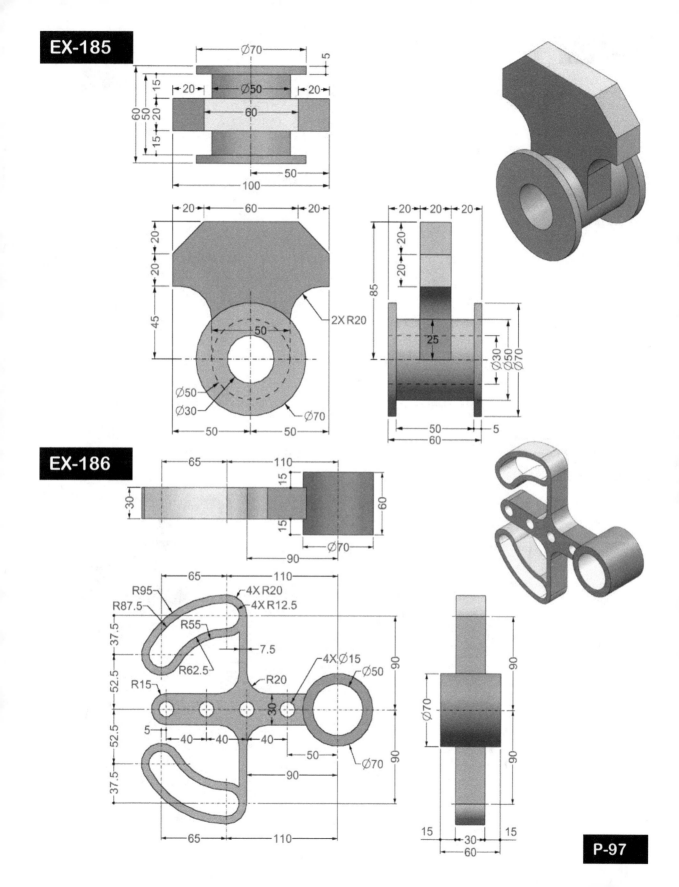

EX-185

⌀70
5
15
20
60
50
20
15
⌀50
60
20
50
100

20
60
20
20
20
20
45
2X R20
⌀50
⌀30
50
50
⌀70

20
20
20
20
20
85
25
⌀30
⌀50
⌀70
50
5
60

EX-186

65
110
15
30
60
15
⌀70
90

65
110
R95
4X R20
R87.5
4X R12.5
37.5
R55
52.5
7.5
R62.5
4X⌀15
⌀50
R15
R20
52.5
30
5
40
40
40
50
90
37.5
⌀70
90
65
110

90
⌀70
90
15
30
15
60

P-97

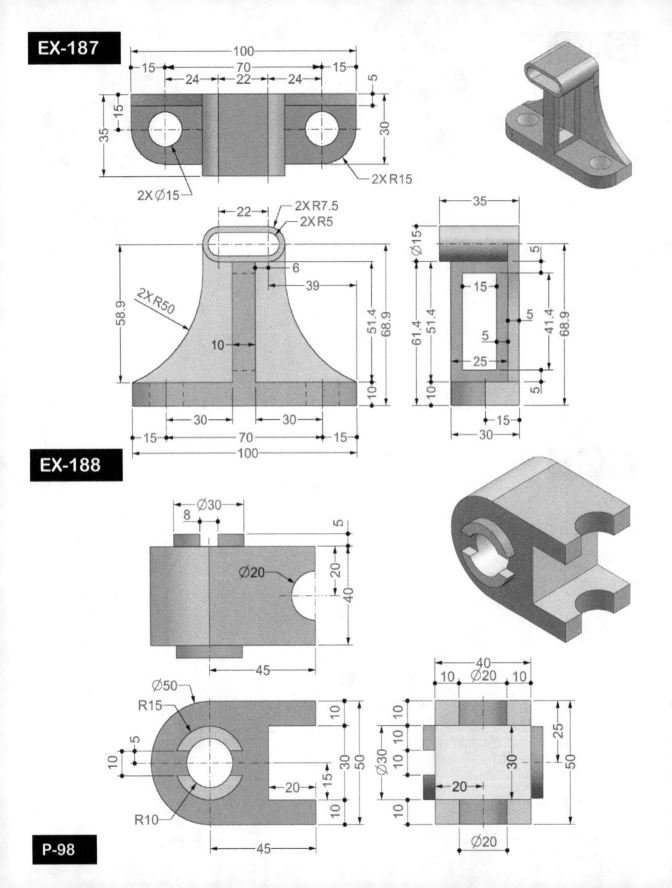

EX-187

100
15
70
15
24
22
24
5
35
15
30
2X R15
2X Ø15

22
2X R7.5
2X R5
6
39
2X R50
58.9
51.4
68.9
10
10
30
30
15
70
15
100

35
Ø15
5
15
61.4
51.4
5
5
41.4
68.9
25
10
5
15
30

EX-188

Ø30
8
5
Ø20
20
40
45

Ø50
R15
5
10
10
20
30
50
15
10
R10
45

40
10   Ø20   10
10
10
25
Ø30
10
30
50
10
20
10
Ø20

P-98

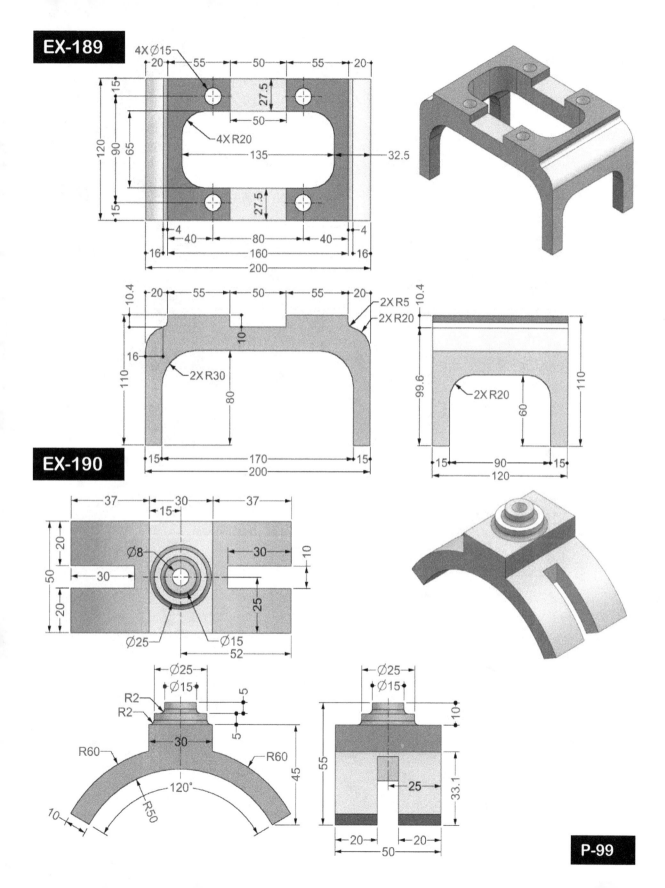

EX-189

EX-190

P-99

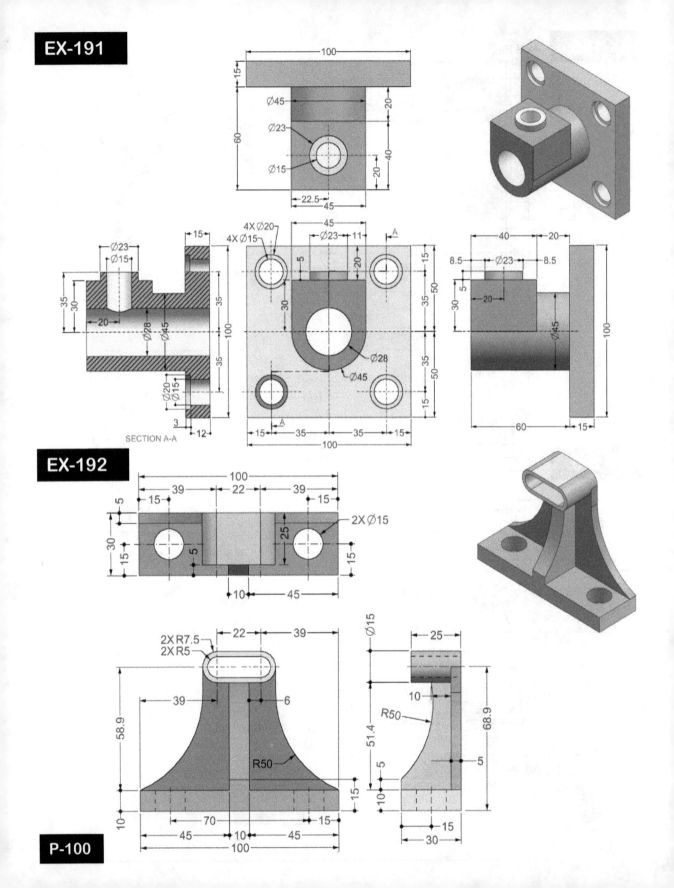

EX-191

100
15
20
Ø45
60
Ø23
40
Ø15
20
22.5
45

SECTION A-A

Ø23
Ø15
35
30
20
Ø28
Ø45
35
35
Ø20
Ø15
100
3
12

45
4X Ø20
4X Ø15
Ø23
11
A
5
20
15
30
50
35
Ø28
35
Ø45
50
15
A
15
35
35
15
100

40
20
8.5
Ø23
8.5
30
5
20
Ø45
100
60
15

EX-192

100
39
22
39
5
15
15
2X Ø15
30
25
15
5
15
10
45

P-100

2X R7.5
2X R5
22
39
Ø15
25
39
6
10
58.9
R50
51.4
R50
5
5
10
15
15
70
15
5
45
10
45
10
15
100
30

EX-193

SECTION A-A

2X Ø14
2X R10
2X Ø8
R20
Ø30
15
Ø30
40
10
Ø20
30
60
30
Ø30
55

Ø20
Ø30
R2
1 x 45°
80
60
10
30
10
Ø8
Ø14

Ø30
Ø23
R2
R2
15
Ø14
40
55
12
10
Ø30

40
Ø30
Ø14
20
R3.2
40
30
30
60
10
12

EX-194

4X Ø20
150
20
110
20
55
40
40
20
R5
130
15
15
30
60
Ø120
40
30
40
70
40
35

ALL HOLES CHAMFER 2MM

130°
2X Ø20
2X Ø50
Ø120
25°
R5
75
PCD Ø160
Ø100
80
R5
40
R5
20
40
70
40
35

60
30
15
80
30
40
R5
20
40
130

70
50
4X Ø20
60
20
20
110
150
BOTTOM VIEW

P-101

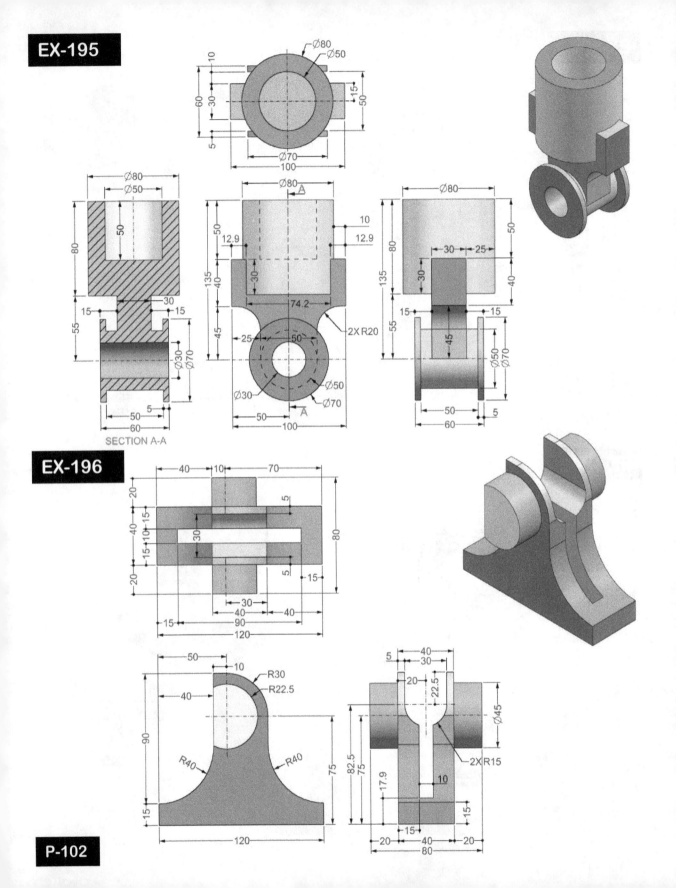

EX-195

Ø80
Ø50
10
60
30
15
50
5
Ø70
100

Ø80
Ø50
50
80
15
30
55
Ø30
Ø70
5
50
60
SECTION A-A

Ø80
A
50
135
40
12.9
30
45
74.2
25
50
2X R20
Ø30
Ø50
Ø70
50
100
A
10
12.9

Ø80
50
80
30 25
135
30
40
15
45
55
Ø50
Ø70
50
5
60

EX-196

40 10 70
20
40
15 10 15
30
15
5
80
5
15
30
40 40
15
90
120
20

50
10
R30
R22.5
40
90
75
R40
R40
15
120

5 40
30
20
22.5
Ø45
82.5
75
2X R15
17.9
10
15
20 40 20
15
80

P-102

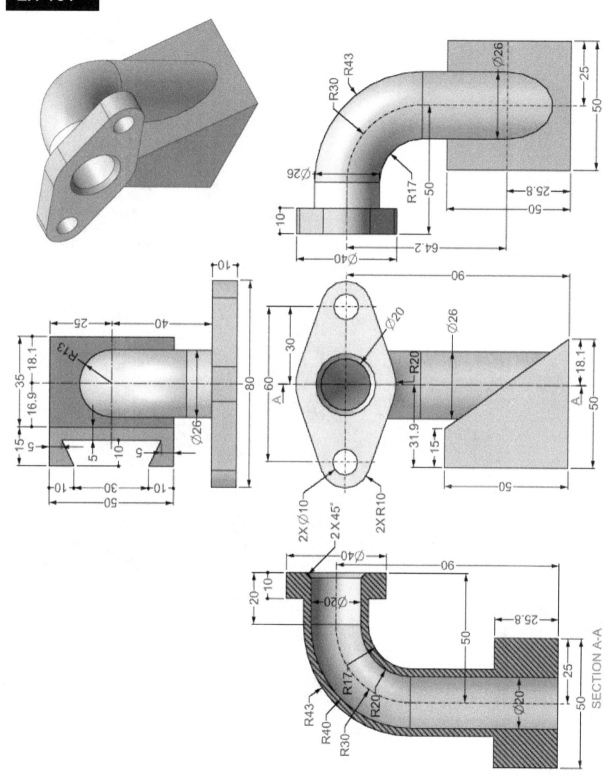

EX-197

P-103

SECTION A-A

6X Ø15THRU
ON PCD 90
Ø120
Ø50
Ø40

PCD Ø90

A
A

120
15
10
Ø15
Ø120
Ø50
Ø40

30

60°
60°

80

Ø10

Ø20
Ø30
PCD 54

5
10

SECTION A-A

B-B

VIEW B-B

Ø20

8X Ø10THRU
ON PCD 54

Ø30
Ø70

PCD Ø54

EX-199

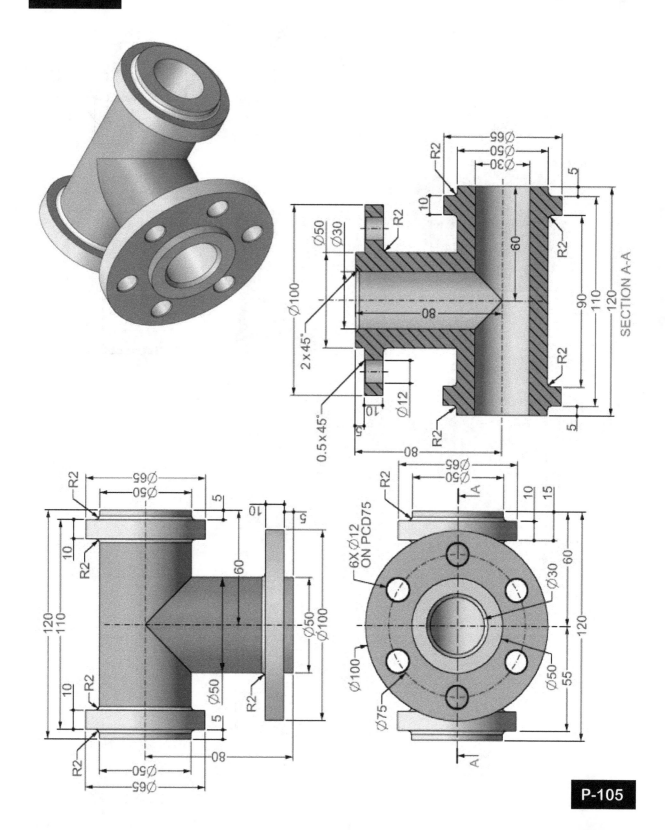

SECTION A-A

Ø65
Ø50
Ø30
R2
10
60
R2
90
110
120
R2
5
5
R2
80

Ø50
Ø30
R2
Ø100
2 x 45°
0.5 x 45°
80
Ø12
10
5

R2
Ø65
Ø50
10
R2
5
120
110
60
10
R2
5
R2
Ø50
Ø65
80
Ø50
Ø100
Ø50
R2

R2
Ø65
Ø50
A
10
15
6X Ø12
ON PCD75
Ø30
60
120
Ø100
55
Ø50
Ø75
A

P-105

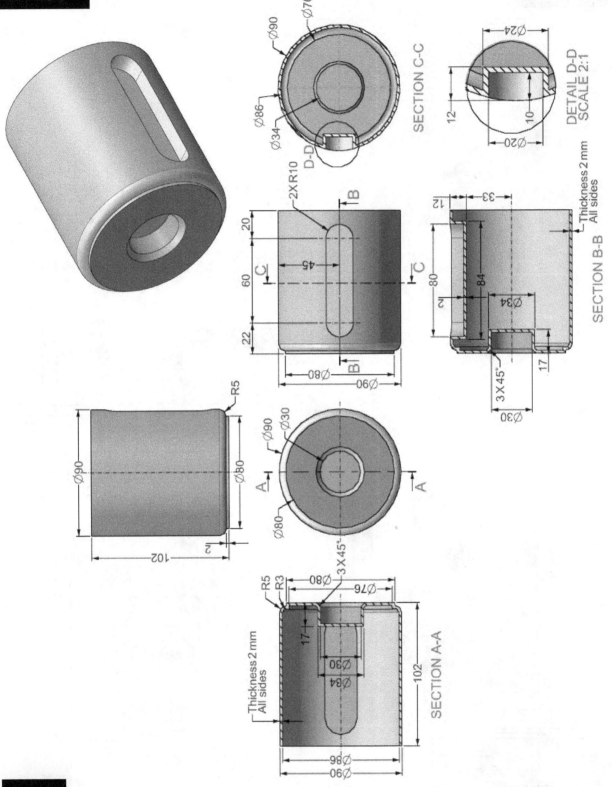

Ø76
Ø90
Ø86
Ø34
D-D
SECTION C-C

Ø24
12
10
Ø20
DETAIL D-D
SCALE 2:1

2X R10
B
20
45
C
60
C
22
B
Ø80
Ø90

12
33
80
42
Ø34
3 X 45°
Ø30
17
Thickness 2 mm
All sides
SECTION B-B

Ø90
Ø80
R5
2
102

Ø90
Ø30
Ø80
A
A
Ø80

R5 R3
Ø80
3 X 45°
17
Ø30
Ø84
102
Thickness 2 mm
All sides
Ø86
Ø90
SECTION A-A

Other useful books by CADIN360

1. 150 CAD Exercises

2. AutoCAD Exercises

3. CAD Exercises

4. 50+ SolidWorks Exercises

5. SolidWorks 200 Exercises

6. Autodesk Inventor Exercises

7. Catia Exercises

8. Siemens NX Exercises